Teaching Slow Learners Through
Active Games

Teaching Slow Learners
Through Active Games

By

JAMES H. HUMPHREY

*Professor of Physical Education
and Health*

DOROTHY D. SULLIVAN

*Associate Professor
of Education*

*University of Maryland
College Park, Maryland*

CHARLES C THOMAS · PUBLISHER

Springfield · Illinois · U.S.A.

Published and Distributed Throughout the World by
CHARLES C THOMAS • PUBLISHER
BANNERSTONE HOUSE
301-327 East Lawrence Avenue, Springfield, Illinois, U.S.A.
NATCHEZ PLANTATION HOUSE
735 North Atlantic Boulevard, Fort Lauderdale, Florida, U.S.A.

Library of Congress Catalog Card Number: 73-126480

With THOMAS BOOKS careful attention is given to all details of
manufacturing and design. It is the Publisher's desire to present books
that are satisfactory as to their physical qualities and artistic possibilities
and appropriate for their particular use. THOMAS BOOKS will be true
to those laws of quality that assure a good name and good will.

Printed in the United States of America

HH-11

Preface

The games movement in education has received widespread recognition in recent years, and increasing attention of educators is being directed to this social psychological phenomenon. The use of games for learning points up a rather decided educational trend supported not only by respectable theoretical postulation but also backed up by sophisticated research.

For the most part, the types of games used in education have been of a passive nature. The present volume is concerned with the types of *learning* games in which children become actively involved. Thus, the learning of academic skills and concepts becomes a part of the child's physical reality. The value of this type of learning experience for slow learners is obvious because of the fact that they deal better with pleasurable concrete experiences than they do with abstract situations.

The first four chapters are concerned with the identification of various types of slow learners, the theory of active game learning, research, and factors influencing learning through active games. The final three chapters contain over two hundred examples of games suitable for use in learning skills and concepts in the areas of reading, elementary school mathematics, and elementary school science.

The book should have a variety of uses. It could be helpful as a text in certain teacher preparation courses in the area of Special Education. In addition, it could serve well as a supplementary text in teacher preparation courses involving Teaching of Reading, Teaching of Elementary School Mathematics, Teaching of Elementary School Science, and Teaching of Elementary School Physical Education. Finally, it should be valuable as a handbook of desirable learning activities and experiences for classroom teachers.

The materials have undergone extensive field trials in various types of school situations. The authors are most grateful to the many teachers who tried out the materials and made valuable suggestions for their use.

College Park, Maryland   J.H.H.
                                                            D.D.S.

CONTENTS

Teaching Slow Learners Through Active Games

Chapter One

The Slow Learning Child

Teach to the individual differences of the learner. This basic principle has led to the development of many components within the educational system. Programs and services are becoming available in school systems that reflect the needs of those with widely varying abilities and interests. Programs and services are being directed to serving citizens of all ages, beginning with the nursery-kindergarten and extending to adult education classes.

Within this broad concept of educational opportunities for our nation's population, there has developed a national concern in recent years for the problems of children with learning impairment. Direct grants for research and service for these children have enabled governmental agencies and private foundations to work cooperatively to help our schools do a better job both in identifying these children and providing more appropriate learning environments for them. The neurologist, the physician, the psychologist, the sociologist, and the researcher in education are contributing new insights into working with these children.

Some of the research in ways children with mental impairment learn provides the teacher with useful guidelines. Research has been directed not only to the etiology, the nature, and the degree of learning impairment but also to the educational environment within which learning takes place for children with such impairment. It is the premise of the authors that the approach to learning through active involvement of the learner is one that needs more recognition and greater emphasis in the learning environment of those children who are identified as *slow learners.* It is the primary purpose of this introductory chapter to discuss the criteria by which children are identified as slow learners and the learning characteristics of these children. Chapters Two, Three, and Four will discuss the theories, the research, and factors influencing learning through active games.

3

WHO IS THE SLOW LEARNER?

While there has been agreement that the needs of children with learning impairment must be reflected in appropriate teaching techniques, there is an increasing awareness of the problems of identification. Too many children in our classrooms have been mistaken for slow learners because of their difficulties in mastering such basic academic skills as reading and arithmetic. It is essential, therefore, that there be a clear understanding of basic differences among children with the *slow learner syndrome* but whose learning problems may be caused by factors other than subnormal intellectual functioning.

The Slow Learner: The Child With Mental Retardation

In the literature the broad generic term *mentally retarded* encompasses all degrees of mental deficit. The designation of the term *slow learner* has been given to those children who have a mild degree (along a continuum) of subnormal intellectual functioning as measured by intelligence tests. The intelligence quotients of these children fall within the range of 70 or 75 to 90. This child in the classroom is making average or below-average progress in the academic skills, depending on where he falls along the continuum of mental retardation. He will probably demonstrate slowness in learning such academic skills as reading and possibly arithmetic. He will very likely have difficulty in the area of the more complex mental processes of defining, analyzing, and comparing. He tends to be a poor reasoner. However, he need not necessarily be equally slow in all aspects of behavior. He may be above average in social adaptability or artistic endeavors.

In respect to physical characteristics, personality, and adjustment, slow-learning children are as variable and heterogeneous as children in the average and above-average range of intellectual potential. Attributes often identified with slow learners are laziness, inattention, and short attention. However, these characteristics are likely to be eliminated when the educational environment is geared to the needs of these children and when there is appropriateness, meaningfulness, and purposefulness to the learning activity.

There is some variance in the literature as to whether these children should be identified as mentally retarded. There is general agreement that the slow learner represents a mild degree of subnormal intellectual functioning whether or not he is labeled mentally retarded. Kirk has described the characteristic education-life patterns of those within the broad educational categories of subnormal intelligence, namely (a) the slow learner, (b) the educable mentally retarded, (c) the trainable mentally retarded, and (d) the totally dependent mentally retarded. With reference to the slow learner he states:

> The slow-learning child is not considered mentally retarded because he is capable of achieving a moderate degree of academic success even though at a slower rate than the average child. He is educated in the regular class program without special provisions except an adaptation of the regular class program to fit his slower learning ability. At the adult level he is usually self-supporting, independent and socially adjusted.[1]

In recent years the dimension of social adaptiveness has gained as an influencing criterion for identification of the mentally retarded. Dywab discusses the criterion of *social acceptance*. He speaks of the growing reluctance to identify persons as mentally retarded on the basis of intellectual subnormality alone:

> Thus a man who scores 65 on an intelligence test and who at the same time shows himself well able to adapt to the social demands of his particular environment at home, at work, and in the community should not be considered retarded. Indeed, we now know that he is not generally so considered.[2]

It is apparent, therefore, that the slow learner with whom the teacher may be working in the classroom may have significant intellectual subnormality.

The Slow Learner: The Child With Depressed Potential

For some years it has been recognized that factors other than intellectual subnormality affected achievement in the classroom. Concern in our schools today for the disadvantaged and culturally

---

[1]Kirk, Samuel A.: *Educating Exceptional Children*. Boston, Houghton Mifflin Company, 1962, pp. 85-86.

[2]Dywab, Gunnar: Who are the mentally retarded? *Children, 15*:44, 1968.

different children is placing increased emphasis on an understanding of these factors. As long as two decades ago these factors were
considered by Featherstone in his delineation of the term *slow
learner*.[3] He differentiated the limited educational achievement
of the *constitutional slow learner* with subnormal intellectual
capacity from the *functional slow learner*. The latter is often mistaken by teachers for a slow learner with limited potential because
he is having difficulty achieving in the classroom. He may be
making limited progress in acquiring the academic skills or he
may be a behavior problem. But his limited achievements are
caused by numerous other factors that serve to depress an individual's ability to learn. Such factors may be the lack of psychosocial
stimulation from limited socioeconomic environment, inadequate
hearing and vision, emotional problems in relationships with
family and peers, malnutrition, or poor general health. It is important to recognize that the situation is not permanent. Both
educational programs and conditions affecting the child's physical,
psychological, or social well-being can be improved.

The Slow Learner: The Child With a Learning Disability

A further compounding of the problem of identification of the
slow learner has occurred with studies of children who do not
come under the categories of the *constitutional* or *functional slow
learner* but whose classroom achievement may be similar. Johnson
and Myklebust warn of the imperative need for proper identification of these children: "Often the child with a learning disability is labeled slow or lazy when in reality he is neither. These
labels have an adverse effect on future learning, on self perception, and on feelings of personal worth."[4]

The research identifying learning-disability children indicates
that their learning has been impaired both in specific areas of
verbal and/or nonverbal learning, but their *potential* for learning
is categorized as normal or above. Thus, these learning-disability

---

[3]Featherstone, W. B.: Teaching the Slow Learner. In Caswell, Hollis L. (Ed.):
Practical Suggestions for Teaching, 2nd ed. New York, Teachers College, Columbia
University, 1951, No. 1, pp. 10-11.

[4]Johnson, Doris J., and Myklebust, Helmer R.: *Learning Disabilities*. New York,
Grune & Stratton, 1967, p. 49.

children fall within the 90 and above IQ range in either the verbal or the nonverbal areas. Total IQ is not used as the criterion for determining learning potential inasmuch as adequate intelligence (either verbal or nonverbal) may be obscured in cases where the total IQ falls below 90 but in which specific aspects of intelligence fall within the definition of adequate intelligence. The learning-disability child whose IQ falls below the normal range and where a learning disability is present, is considered to have a multiple involvement.

In learning-disability children there are deficits in verbal and/or nonverbal learning. There may be impairment of expressive, receptive, or integrative functions. There is concern for deficits in the function of input and output, of sensory modalities and overloading, and of degree of impairment. The essential differences of the mentally retarded and the learning-disability child have been characterized as the following:

> One cannot deny that the neurology of learning has been disturbed in the mentally retarded, but the fundamental effect has been to reduce potential for learning in general. Though some retarded children have isolated *high* levels of function, the pattern is one of generalized inferiority; normal potential for learning is *not* assumed. In comparison, children with learning disabilities have isolated *low* levels of function. The pattern is one of generalized integrity of mental capacity; normal potential *is* assumed.[5]

Consequently, the learning-disability child shows marked differences from the child with limited potential. There are both qualitative and quantitative differences. The learning-disability child has more potential for learning. The means by which he learns are different.

While there may be some overlapping in the educational methods used with these three groups identified as *slow learners,* there obviously must be differentiation in educational goals and approaches for these various groups. Correct identification of the factors causing *slowness in learning* is essential in teaching to the individual differences of children. The theories and practices presented in the following chapters outline an effective approach

---

[5]*Ibid.,* p. 55.

for teachers to use in working with the child most appropriately identified as the *constitutional slow learner*. However, it is recognized that the active approach to learning through games is also very appropriate in many situations for those children with learning problems caused by factors other than subnormal intellectual functioning.

LEARNING CHARACTERISTICS OF THE SLOW LEARNER

When considering educational processes that would provide a successful learning experience for the children with limited intellectual potential, it is necessary to examine some of their basic characteristics of learning as found from numerous studies. *Slow learners* appear to follow the same patterns as those who have more adequate intellectual endowment in terms of the sequence of growth and development. The basic difference is the time schedule at which these children arrive at various levels of development. Theoretically, the child with an IQ of 80 develops intellectually at a rate only four-fifths that of the average child. The rate of development of these children is more closely correlated with their mental age than their chronological age.

Johnson, in his summation of the research on the learning characteristics of the mentally retarded, emphasizes that they learn in the same way as normal children. The studies indicate "remarkable agreement in the results, regardless of the environment or degree of intellectual deficit."[6] As yet, significant differences have not been found between normal and retarded groups in serial learning, verbal mediation, repetitive learning, and transfer of learning. At the present time the research has not supported the theory that the mentally retarded require more time to learn a specific task when compared with the normal child. Johnson concludes:

> Although the two groups (normal and mentally handicapped) may differ significantly on such developmental factors as life age, physical and motor development, or social development, as long as they are equated for intellectual developmental levels,

---

[6]Johnson, C. Orville: Psychological characteristics of the mentally retarded. In Cruikshank, William M. (Ed.): *Psychology of Exceptional Children and Youth*, 2nd ed. Englewood Cliffs, Prentice-Hall, Inc., 1963, p. 457.

experiences, and previous learnings to ensure equal readiness, they should have similar patterns of learning, require the same amounts of practice, and retain equal amounts of the material learned.[7]

Differences have been found in comparison of the learning processes in arithmetic and reading of the mentally retarded and normal children. However, according to Johnson these differences are *not* attributable to *ability* to learn but to the influence of instructional procedures. Included among the factors affecting the learning process are the value systems of the individual and his own concept of self as a learner. These two factors must be recognized as particularly important. The reason for this is that there are so many negative psychosocial factors operating within the life space of large percentages of the mentally retarded who can maintain themselves only in a low socioeconomic environment.

Kirk's studies relating to the effect of preschool education on the development of educable mentally retarded children clearly show that school experience can make a difference on rate of development.

> It would appear that although the upper limits of development for an individual are genetically or organically determined, the functional level or rate of development may be accelerated or depressed within the limits set by the organism. Somatopsychological factors and the cultural milieu (including schooling) are capable of influencing the functional level within these limits.[8]

In providing appropriate learning experiences for slow learners, it is essential to help them be successful by structuring activities to reflect the best principles of learning. According to Kirk these principles are the following:

1. Progress is from the known to the unknown, using concrete materials to foster understanding of more abstract facts. (Use of active games helps children act out and see the concepts being developed.)*

2. The child is helped to transfer known abilities from one

---

[7]*Ibid.* p. 461.

[8]Kirk, Samuel A.: *Op. Cit.* pp. 100-101.

*Parentheses are authors.

situation to another rather than being expected to make generalizations spontaneously. (Movement-oriented active games enable children to work out the relationship of one situation with another and to make appropriate transfer of skills and generalizations easily.)

3. The teacher uses many repetitions in a variety of experiences. (Active games provide a pleasurable, highly motivating means for necessary repetition.)

4. Learning is stimulated through exciting situations. (Personal involvement, high interest, and motivation are concomitant with learning through active games.)

5. Inhibitions are avoided by presenting one idea at a time and presenting learning situations by sequential steps. (The structure of active games in itself implies logical ordering of ideas that are dramatized through physical movement.)

6. Learning is reinforced through using a variety of sense modalities—visual, vocal, auditory, kinesthetic.[9] (Motor learning heightens the learning act when integrated with verbal learning experiences.)

Such guidelines emphasize the need for total involvement of the learner, for using the concrete experience to develop an abstract concept, and for providing for continuity and transference of one learning experience to another. A good many years ago Featherstone also stressed the need for working with the concrete:

> One of the chief reasons for emphasizing activities based upon very concrete and tangible or objective things rather than upon predominantly verbal or abstract things is that such activities usually permit more demonstrating, constructing, picturing, and dramatizing as means of communicating ideas.[10]

Such techniques are more likely to ensure successful learning for all children, regardless of intellectual potential; for slow learners they are essential. The use of active games to develop abstract concepts in reading, elementary-school mathematics, and science are therefore sound methodology for all learners and particularly appropriate for the slow learner.

---

[9]*Ibid.* p. 121.
[10]Featherstone, W. B.: *Op. Cit.*, p. 66.

Chapter Two

Theory of Learning Through Active Games

The important role of play and games in cognition and learning has been recognized for centuries. In fact, the idea of the playing of games as a desirable learning medium has been traced to the ancient Egyptians. Through the ages some of the most profound thinkers in history have expounded positively in terms of the value of games as a way of learning. Perhaps one of the earliest pronouncements in this regard was Plato's suggestion that ". . . in teaching children; train them by a kind of game and you will be able to see more clearly the natural bent of each."

In modern times there has been a revival of the *play way* of learning among some educators and psychologists. Much of this has tended to center around certain educational games more or less *passive* in nature. The approach in the present volume is concerned essentially with those types of games which are *active* in nature. Therefore, throughout the text the term *games* will imply *active interaction of children in cooperative and/or competitive situations.* In other words, when we speak of *active* games as a learning medium, we refer to things that children *do* actively in a pleasurable social situation in order to learn. This concept of active games is in agreement with the basic educational principle that learning is always an individual matter but that it takes place most effectively in a social setting. Two important aspects concerned with this principle are that (a) a group can stimulate individual activity, and (b) individuals in a group can learn vicariously from each other. Active games provide an outstanding setting for this type of situation.

The active game approach to learning is concerned with how children can develop skills and concepts in such school subject areas as reading, mathematics, and science while actively engaged in game situations. Although all children differ in one or more

11

characteristics, the fact remains that they are more *alike* than they are different. The one common likeness of all children is that they all move; they live in a movement world, so to speak. The active game approach to learning is based essentially on the theory that children will learn better when what might be called *academic learning* takes place through pleasurable physical activity; that is, when the *motor* component operates at a maximal level in skill and concept development in school subject areas traditionally oriented to *verbal* learning. This is *not* to say that *motor* and *verbal* learning are two mutually exclusive kinds of learning, although it has been suggested that at the two extremes the dichotomy appears justifiable. It is recognized that in verbal learning, which involves almost complete abstract symbolic manipulations, there may be, among others, such motor components as tension, subvocal speech, and physiological changes in metabolism which operate at a minimal level. It is also recognized that in active games where the learning is predominantly motor in nature, verbal learning is evident, although perhaps at a minimal level. For example, in teaching an active game, there is a certain amount of verbalization in developing a kinesthetic concept of or *kinesthetic feel* for the particular game that is being taught.

The active game approach to learning is also concerned with other elements that are inherent in the participation of active games. Two such elements involve *motivation,* particularly as it relates to interest, and certain principles of *reinforcement.* All of these factors will be discussed in detail in a subsequent chapter and are mentioned here only as a means of identifying the theoretical aspect of the active game approach to learning.

The procedure of learning through active games involves the selection of an active game which is taught to the children and used as a learning activity for the development of a skill or concept in a specific subject area. An attempt is made to arrange an active learning situation so that a fundamental intellectual skill or concept is being practiced in the course of participating in the active game situation. Activities are selected on the basis of the degree of inherence of a skill or concept in a given school subject area, as well as the appropriate physical ability and social level

of a given group of children. In order to give the reader some
insight into this type of learning activity, a number of representative examples are included in the ensuing section of this chapter.

EXAMPLES OF ACTIVE GAME LEARNING SITUATIONS

The representative examples of active game learning situations
presented here include two from each of the elementary school
subject areas of reading, mathematics, and science. In the chapters
specifically designated for these subject areas, many such examples
will be presented.

The first two examples involve active game learning situations
which are designed to help children learn certain skills which are
important in reading. The first of these concerns a reading skill:
To distinguish between words that use the *c* or *s* in making the *s*
sound. The game to develop the skill is called *C's* and *S's* which
is an adaptation of the game Crows and Cranes, as shown in the
following diagram:

The children are divided equally into two groups, the *C's* and
the *S's*, who line up facing each other, with their lines about five
feet apart. A goal line is drawn a given distance behind each
group. The teacher calls out a word that is spelled with either
a *c* or an *s*. If the word requires a *c*, all of the *C's* run to reach
their goal line before being tagged by a member of the *S's* group.
All of those tagged become members of the opposite group. The
groups then return to their respective lines, and the same procedure
is followed with another word. The group having the greater
number of players on its side at the end of a specified playing
time is the winner.

The next example involves a phonics skill: Auditory perception of long and short vowels. The activity used to develop this

skill is an adaptation of the game Steal the Bacon, as shown in the following diagram:

Team A	Team B
ā	u
ē	o
ī	i
ō	e
ū	a

Bacon

a	ū
e	ō
i	ī
o	ē
u	ā

Two teams face each other about fifteen feet apart. An object (the bacon) is placed in the middle of the space between the two lines. The members of both teams are given like vowels, some with a short sound and some with a long sound. The teacher calls out a word with a short vowel, such as *flash, hit,* or *bet,* or a word containing a long vowel, such as *rode, wave,* or *shade.* The two children on each team who have the correct vowel sound run out and try to grab the object and return it to their line. If the player does so, his team scores two points, and if he is tagged by his opponent in the process, the opposing team scores one point. For example, if the teacher calls the word "cave," the child with the long ā on one team and the child with the long ā on the other team would try to retrieve the object. The children should be identified periodically with different letters.

The next example is concerned with a mathematics concept: Separating groups and comparing groups and grouping of three. The activity to develop the concept is the game Squirrels in Trees. It is conducted in the following manner: With the exception of one player the children are arranged in groups of three. Two of the players in each group of three face each other and hold hands, forming a *hollow tree.* The third player is a *squirrel* and stands between the other two in the hollow tree. The extra player, who is also a squirrel, stands near the center of the playing area. The leader calls "Change!" On this signal all squirrels must get into a different hollow tree, and the extra squirrel also tries to find a tree. There will always be one squirrel left who does not have a tree. In developing the concept, the children are numbered *one's, two's,* and *three's.* Numbers *one* and *two* are the trees. Number *three's* are the squirrels for the first few times. Then the numbers are alternated so that number *one's* and *two's* can be squirrels. This way the children can see that the groups continue to be *three's* even though they change position and name a number of times.

The next example involves a mathematics concept: Dividing to find how many groups there are in a larger group. The activity to develop this concept is the game Get Together. In this game the players take places around the activity area in a scattered formation. The teacher calls any number by which the total number of players is not exactly divisible. All players try to form groups of the number called. Each of these groups join hands in a circle. The one or ones left out may have points scored against them. After a specified period of playing time, the child with the lowest score can be declared the winner. The numbers called should be those with which a particular group of children is learning to divide. For example, with a normal group at third-grade level, the numbers might be 2, 3, 4, 5, or 10. This activity is useful for reinforcing the idea of groups or sets and that groups are of like things (in this case children). It can give the children the idea that there may be a *remainder* when dividing into groups.

The following example is for developing a science concept: Things which are balanced have equal weights on either side of their central point. The activity to develop this concept is Rush and Tug. In this game there are two groups, with each group standing behind one of two parallel lines which are about forty feet apart. In the middle of these two parallel lines, a rope is laid perpendicular to them. A cloth is tied to the center of the rope to designate both halves of the rope. On a signal members of both groups rush to their half of the rope, pick it up, and tug toward the group's end line. The group pulling the midpoint of the rope past its own end line in a specified amount of time is declared the winner. If at the end of the designated time the midpoint of the rope has not been pulled beyond one group's end line, the group with the midpoint of the rope nearer to its end line is declared the winner.

In performing this activity, the groups can experiment with all kinds of combinations of teams such as boys versus boys, girls versus girls, boys versus girls, larger children against smaller children, and mixed sizes and weights against the same. This activity presents a genuine problem-solving situation as they try to get the exact combination of children for an equal balance of the two teams. When there is enough experimenting, two teams of equal proportions may be assembled, and they will likely find that it is most difficult for either to make any headway. They also are likely to discover that an equal balance depends not only on the weight of their classmates but a great extent upon their strength.

The final example presented here is concerned with a science concept: Electricity travels along a pathway and needs a complete circuit over which to travel. The activity to develop the concept is Straddle Ball Roll. The group is divided into four or more smaller groups. The children of each group stand one behind the other in single file. All are in a stride position, with feet far enough apart so that a ball can be rolled between the legs of the players. The first person in each file holds a rubber playground ball. At a signal the person in front of each file starts the activity by attempting to roll the ball between the legs of all the children in his file. The team that gets the ball to the last member of the file first in the manner described scores a point. The last player goes to the head of his file, and this procedure is continued, with a point scored each time for the team that gets the ball back to the last player first. After every player has had an opportunity to roll the ball back, the team which has scored the most points is declared the winner. An application of this would be as follows: The first player at the head of each file becomes the electric switch which opens and shuts the circuit. The ball is the electric current. As the ball rolls between the children's legs, it moves right through if all legs are in proper lineup. When a leg is not in the proper stride, the path of the ball is impeded, and the ball rolls out. The game has to be stopped until the ball is recovered and the corection made in the position of the leg. The circuit (that is the child's leg) has to be repaired before the flow of electricity (which is the path of the ball) can be resumed.

It should be clearly understood that a specific application be made with the active game to the particular learning situation. This is to say that learning will not necessarily take place automatically and that relationships, inferences, and the like should be made during the teaching situation. The following tape-recorded teacher-pupil discussion of a play party game should help to illustrate this point.

Teacher: Boys and girls, when reading about sports events in the paper the other day, I came across some sentences that I thought would be of interest to you. In a story about a baseball game, one sentence said, "The baserunner *danced* back and forth off of first base." In another report about a football game, there was a sentence that said, "The halfback *danced* down the field." As I thought about this it occurred to me that dancing might be a good way to develop some of the skills needed to play well in sport and games. Have any of you ever heard of how rhythm and dancing could help to make better players?

Pupil 1: Gee, I never thought of it that way before.

Pupil 2: Me, either.

Teacher: Please form a large circle with a boy and girl in every other place. (Pupils form the circle.) Today we are going to learn a dance called "Pop Goes the Weasel." Probably many of you have heard the tune before. Let me see the hands of those who have. (Some pupils indicate that they are familiar with the tune.) Do you remember the other day when we were studying fractions, what we said the bottom number told us?

Pupil 3: I think it is how many parts something is divided into.

Teacher: Yes, that's right, and now we are going to divide our large circle into groups of three. Starting here, we will form small circles with three persons in each small circle with hands joined. (Teacher demonstrates with first group of three to her left.) Now, each group is a circle made up of three persons. If something is divided into three parts, what do we call the name of each part?

Pupil 4: One-third?

Teacher: Yes, that's right. Can someone tell me how many thirds make a whole?

Pupil 5: Three.

Pupil 6: (Aside to **Pupil 7**) Oh! I see now what she meant the other day.

Teacher: Alright. Now let's have each person in the small circles take the name of either First-Third, Second-Third, or Last-Third. Just take a minute to decide within your own circle who will take each part. (Teacher demonstrates with one of the small circles.) Let me see the hands of all the First-Thirds, the Second-Thirds, the Last-Thirds. Now, here is something that is very important. The magic word in this dance is *pop*. That is, if the words of the tune were to be sung. We will move to the right in our own circles. When we come to the part of the music where the word *Pop* would be sung, the person in each circle with the name First-Third will pop under the arms of the other two persons in his circle and become a part of the circle to his right. The people in the small circles will immediately begin to walk again, and this time on the word *pop*, the person named Second-Third will leave his circle. The next time, the person named Last-Third leaves. Who do you think will pop the next time?

Pupil 1: Would we start all over again with First-Third?

Teacher: Yes, that's right, and we will continue that way until the record has finished playing. I am going to play a part of the record for you. This time I want you to listen to the music, and when you hear the part where you pop into the next circle, raise your hand so that we can make sure that you will know when to pop. That's fine. Everyone seems to know when to pop. Listen for the chord to start. (Pupils participate in the dance, and after the record is played through once, the teacher evaluates the activity with them.)

Teacher: What were some of the things you noticed that you thought were good about our first atempt at this dance?

Pupil 2: We all seemed to go in the right direction and didn't get mixed up.

Pupil 3: We kept time pretty well.

Teacher: What are some of the things you like about it?

Pupil 4: I liked being in a different circle.

Pupil 6: Well, it made me catch on to fractions better.

Pupil 7: Me too. We ought to do arithmetic that way all the time.

Teacher: You think it was easier to learn fractions that way?

Pupil 6: I'll say, and it was lots more fun.

Teacher: What are some of the ways we might improve it if we tried it another time?

Pupil 1: We ought to try to all pop at the same time.

Pupil 2: Maybe we shouldn't try to go around the circle so fast.

Teacher: Yes, those are good suggestions. Personally, I think it was rather well done for our first attempt.

VALUE OF THE ACTIVE GAME MEDIUM WITH SLOW LEARNERS

One of the important research findings of the active game learning medium is concerned with its positive effect on slow-learning children. Perhaps the primary reason for this is that slow learners do not necessarily tend to deal too well with the more abstract kinds of learning situations inherent in many of the traditional school procedures. On the contrary, the active game learning medium involves a much more meaningful kind of experience for the child. The learning environment is such that the child actually has a direct, purposeful, and pleasurable experience when participating in an active game. The representative illustrations that follow should point this up more clearly.

Case 1

In using the game Straddle Ball Roll (described earlier) with with a heterogeneous group of fourth-grade children to develop the concept that electricity travels along a pathway and needs a complete circuit over which to travel, the following was observed:

The children quickly made the analogy themselves after noticing how interference in the path of the ball caused it to go out of bounds and stop the game. In a similar manner, blockage of an electric current would break the circuit and stop the flow of electricity.

An experiment with wired batteries and a bell had also been used in connection with the development of this concept. Three of the slower learning children reported that they understood this better after they had played Straddle Ball Roll because they could actually *see* the electric current, which in this case was the ball.

Case 2

In a special education class the teacher attempted to develop the concept of self body image through a game called Busy Bee. In this game the children are in pairs facing each other and dispersed around the activity area. One child who is the *caller* is in the center of the area. He makes calls such as "shoulder to shoulder," "toe to toe," or "hand to hand." (In the early stages of the game it was necessary for the teacher to do the calling.) As the calls are made, the paired children go through the appropriate motions with their partners. After a few calls the caller will shout "Busy Bee!" This is the signal for every child to get a new partner, including the caller. The child who does not get a partner can become the new caller.

As the children played the game, the teacher made them aware of the location of various parts of their body in order to develop the concept of full body image.

Before the game was played, the children were asked to draw a picture of themselves. Many did not know how to begin, and others omitted some of the major limbs in their drawings. After playing Busy Bee, the children were again asked to draw a picture of themselves. This time they were more successful. All of the drawings had bodies, heads, arms, and legs. Some of them had hands, feet, eyes, and ears. A few even had teeth and hair.

Case 3

This illustration involved a class of fourteen children, nine years two months to twelve years two months of age, with an IQ range from 60 to 85. Two examples of games used with this class follow:

In the first game the teacher was attempting to develop a better understanding of addition facts. The game used for this purpose was Exchange Numbers. Seven 6 by 8 inch index cards are used with a number from six to twelve on one side of each. On the other side are written the combinations which, when added together, give the sum of the number on the opposite side. For example, if the number on one side were twelve, then the combinations on the other side would be

6	7	8	9	10	11	12
6	5	4	3	2	1	0
—	—	—	—	—	—	—

A duplicate set of these cards is made. Each pupil is given a card, with two pupils having identical cards. The leader stands in front of the class and calls out two numbers. The pupils having the sum of these two numbers try to exchange places before being tagged by the leader. After playing the game for a time, a new leader can be selected, or the person tagged may become the leader.

The pupils made the cards during the regular arithmetic class and were told that they were to be used later during a play period in a new game. Numbers from six to twelve were given to the pupils, with two pupils having the same number. The class was paired off, with the two pupils who had the same number being together. The pairs went to the chalkboard to work out the combinations which, when added together, gave the sum of their respective numbers. Then they checked their answers for accuracy on the abacus, with the teacher giving guidance as needed. They returned to their desks to make the cards. Each pupil made one card.

The game was explained and played during the play period which, because of rain, had to take place in the classroom. The leader called two numbers, and the two pupils having the sum of the two numbers stood and attempted to change seats before being tagged. The pupil tagged became *It*. One of the problems that arose in the game was that sometimes one child would understand the combination before the other. He would have no place to run to and would be tagged because the other child did not move from his seat. To correct this, it was decided that the runner could stand and touch the back of his chair and be safe until the other person stood up. The leader had to stay in front of the room until someone left his seat.

In evaluating this activity, it was observed that the preparation for the activity gave experience in addition and writing numbers and that the children were more motivated to do this when they found they were going to use the cards in a game. The pupils saw a purpose in learning the addition facts and in checking for accuracy as well as making legible figures. They also had a better understanding of *pairs* and *exchange*. The fact that a pleasurable use for the addition facts was created was valuable. The pupils were aware that listening was important, that it was necessary to run and dodge quickly, and that they had to be careful to avoid running into each other. They enjoyed the avtivity very much and asked to play the game during indoor recess.

The second example with this class was concerned with recognition of beginning sounds. The game used for this purpose was a version of Steal the Bacon, the class was divided into two teams of seven each and stood ten feet apart, facing each other. The members on both teams were given the letter *b, c, d, h, m, n,* and *p* as in the following diagram because the class had been having difficulty with the beginning consonants.

b		*p*
c		*n*
d		*m*
h	beanbag	*h*
m	(bacon)	*d*
n		*c*
p		*b*

The teacher called out a word such as *ball,* and the two pupils having the letter *b* ran out to grab the beanbag. If the player got the beanbag back to his line, he scored two points for his team. If his opponent tagged him before he got back, the other team scored one point. The game ended when each letter had been called. After the scores were totalled, the game was repeated at the request of the children. When the game was continued, the children were identified with different letters.

In evaluating this activity, the children pointed out that listening was important in order to understand the letter called. This was particularly necessary to distinguish the sounds of *b* and *d* and *m* and *n*. It was also necessary to run and dodge rapidly in order to achieve the goal. They also mentioned that they had to know about addition in order to keep score.

Case 4

In this illustration two groups of fifth-grade children were equated by matched pairs on the basis of pretest scores on science concepts.[1] One group was designated as the active game group, and the other was designated as the conventional group. The IQ range of the active game group was from 74 to 89, with a mean of 85. The conventional group's IQ range was from 72 to 90, with a mean of 83. The children were tested three times. After the first test had been administered to a large group, ten matched pairs were selected. Both groups were taught the same science concepts by the same teacher, one through conventional procedures and the other by active games. The teaching was over a two-week period, at which time the children were retested. Following this second test there was no formal instruction on the science concepts that were taught during this two-week period. They were tested a third time for retention at an interval of three months after the second test. The following arrays of scores show the results of all three tests for all pupils:

---

[1]Humphrey, James H.: A comparison of the use of the active game learning medium and traditional learning media in the development of fifth grade science concepts with children with below normal intelligence quotients. *Research Abstracts.* Washington, D. C., American Association for Health, Physical Education and Recreation, 1970.

Conventional Group				*Active Game Group*			
Pupil	*Test 1*	*Test 2*	*Test 3*	*Pupil*	*Test 1*	*Test 2*	*Test 3*
A	43	23	40	A	43	73	73
B	23	43	43	B	23	60	67
C	37	33	37	C	37	63	73
D	50	63	60	D	50	73	90
E	53	63	50	E	53	73	83
F	47	57	60	F	47	60	70
G	47	47	53	G	47	77	63
H	33	53	40	H	33	60	67
I	50	77	63	I	50	90	87
J	33	43	57	J	33	70	60
Total	416	502	503	*Total*	416	699	733
Mean	41.6	50.2	50.3	*Mean*	41.6	69.9	73.3

The difference in mean scores was used as the criterion for learning. When analyzed statistically, it was found that the active game group learned significantly more than the conventional group. Also, the active game group showed a high level of retention for the three-month period. Although the conventional group retained what was learned, the gain in learning was minimal to begin with.

It is very interesting to note that the two groups in this experiment resembled very closely a type of slow learner identified by Lanning and Robbins.[2] They have suggested that typically the slow learner has an IQ range from 95 down to 75. They also assert that he may have below average health, with the most common physical problems being hearing and vision defects. In addition, he may not have the level of curiosity or creativity of other pupils, and although he can develop reasoning skills, he is not likely to do so unless given the opportunity to utilize problem solving. In this regard, it appears significant that in addition to the quantitative data reported above, there was observable evidence of many more opportunities for reasoning and problem solving in the experiences of the active game group than for the group taught by conventional procedures. Another important factor was the meaningfulness and motivation connected with the active game learning experiences.

---

[2]Lanning, Frank, and Robbins, Russell: The slow learner. *The Instructor*, 77:183; 1967.

CURRENT STATUS AND FUTURE PROSPECTS OF THE ACTIVE GAME LEARNING MEDIUM

One of the reasons given for studying the history of a subject is that it helps to determine how the past has challenged the present, so that we might better understand how the present might challenge the future. As far back as the early Greeks, it was suggested by Plato that "learning takes place better through play and play situations." Similar pronouncements made over the years include those by Aristotle, Quintillian, Rousseau, Froebel, and Dewey. Despite many esteemed endorsements of the game approach to learning, there is not a great deal of historical evidence that indicates that there was widespread practice of it in the schools. Pestalozzi, the noted Swiss educator, who is sometimes credited with laying the foundation for modern teaching, was an exponent of the idea in his own school. Later Friedrich Froebel, who is considered the founder of the kindergarten, perhaps incorporated the practice as a part of the school day. Perhaps, having been influenced by some of his predecessors, Dewey indicated his thought on the matter in 1919 with reference to this approach to learning in the actual school situation. He commented that "Experience has shown that when children have a chance at physical activities which bring their natural impulses into play, going to school is a joy, management is less of a burden, and learning is easier.[3]

In more recent times the use of games in education has been given considerable atention. A concrete example of this is a statement made in the publication *The Shape of Education for 1966-67.* In a chapter entitled "Learning is Child's Play," referring to games in education, the following comment is made: "And the University of Maryland has a professor of physical education and health, James H. Humphrey, who has devised a whole series of playground games teaching the elements of language, science, arithmetic and such matters to elementary school children." Further, "The strange thing about all these incidents is that they are isolated and unrelated but that they demonstrate an educational trend for

---

[3]Dewey, John: *Democracy and Education, An Introduction to the Philosophy of Education.* New York, The Macmillan Co., 1919, pp. 228-229.

which there is respectable theoretical justification in serious academic research."[4]

It seems worthy of mention that in contemporary society there is a certain degree of universality in the use of active games for learning. While the ideologies of the Eastern and Western worlds may differ in many respects, apparently there is some agreement about this approach to learning. For example, Edward Hunter reports the following in his book *Brain-Washing in Red China:*

> There was even an arithmetic game in which there were two teams of fifteen players each and an umpire. Ten students on each side would represent a number from one to ten, and the other five players would represent the symbols used in arithmetic; plus (+); minus (—); division (÷); multiplication (×); and equals (=). The umpire would shout out an example, such as two times four minus eight equals zero, and each side would rush to line up in this order. The team to do so first was the winner.[5]

In a somewhat similar frame of reference, the Russian Ivanitchkii, has stated, "Teachers of mathematics and physics should use examples of sports in solving problems."[6]

Up to this point, we have only been extrolling the rectitude of the active game approach to learning. Certainly we would be remiss if we did not call attention to some of its possible limitations. However, the suggested limitations of it are likely to center around inertia of individuals and tradition rather than the validity of the medium itself. In any event, some people in education may feel that pupils will not take active games seriously enough as a way of learning and therefore will not concentrate on the skill or concept being taught. However, our personal experience with this medium has been quite the contrary. In another sense, some may fear that active games as a way of learning may be *too* attrac-

4Editors of *EDUCATION U. S. A., The Shape of Education for 1966-67.* Washington, D. C., National School Public Relations Association, 1966, p. 49.

5Hunter, Edward: *Brain-Washing in Red China.* New York, The Vanguard Press, 1951, p. 46.

6Ivanitchskii, M. F.: Physical education of school children—the constant concern of all pedagogical collectives. *Theory and Practice of Physical Culture,* 4:10, 1962 (Russian). From an abstract by Michael Yessis, *Research Quarterly, 35:*339, 1964.

tive to pupils. For example, in many of our experiments some children have asked, "Why don't we learn it this way all the time?"

It should be pointed out very forcefully here that we do not necessarily recommend that active game learning be the tail that wags the "educational dog." But, rather we would like to look upon it as *another* valid way that children might learn and not necessarily the only way. We are well aware of the fact that everything cannot be taught best through active games, simply because all children do not learn in the same way.

Although it is difficult to predict what the future holds for the active game learning medium, we feel pretty well assured that more serious attention is currently being paid to it. Discussions with leading neurophysiologists, learning theorists, child development specialists, and others reveal a positive feeling toward the active game learning medium. And there is pretty general agreement that the premise is very sound from all standpoints: philosophical, physiological, and psychological.

Chapter Three

Research in Active Game Learning

It was mentioned in Chapter Two that learning through physical activity is not a recent innovation. In fact, over the years the literature on this subject has been replete with pronouncements of eminent philosophers and educators. The favorable comments of such people obviously carry a great deal of weight. However. in an age when so much emphasis is placed upon scientific inquiry and research, we cannot accept only the subjective opinions of even some of history's most profound thinkers; thus, the necessity to place an objective base under a long-held theoretical postulation.

RESEARCH TECHNIQUES

There are many satisfactory ways of studying how behavioral changes take place in children. In our work in this area one of the first problems to be reckoned with was whether this type of learning activity could be accomplished in the regular school situation and also whether teachers whose training and experience had been predominantly in traditional methods would subscribe to this particular approach. To obtain this information, a procedure that could best be described as *nautralistic observation* was used. This involved the teaching of a skill or concept to a group of children by an active game in which the skill or concept was inherent. The teacher would then evaluate how well the skill or concept was learned through the active game learning medium. The teacher's criteria for evaluation were his or her past experiences with other groups of children and other learning media. Scores of these types of observations were made at all elementary school grade levels in most of the regular school subject areas.

Naturally, this procedure is grossly lacking in objectivity because there is only a subjective evaluation of the teacher to support the hypotheses. However, in the early stages of the work, this technique served our purpose well because at that time we were mainly concerned with having teachers experiment with the idea and to ascertain their reactions to it. In a vast majority of cases the reactions of teachers were very positive.

The next factor that needed to be taken into consideration was whether or not children could *actually* learn through the active game medium. Although for centuries empirical evidence had placed the hypothesis in a very positive position, there was still the need for some objective evidence to support the hypothesis. In order to determine if learning could actually take place through active games, the *single group technique* was employed. This technique involved the criterion measure of objective pretesting of a group of children on certain skills or concepts in a specific curriculum area. Active games in which skills or concepts were inherent were taught to the children over a specified period of time and used as learning activities to develop the skills or concepts. After the specified period of time the children were retested and served as their own controls for comparing results of the second test with the results of the pretest.

All of our studies involving this technique in which the subjects were their own control have shown significant differences between pretest and post-test scores at a very high level of probability. Therefore, it appeared reasonable to conclude that learning actually could take place through the active game medium.

With the above information at hand, the next and obviously the most important step was to determine how the active game medium compared with other more traditional learning media. For this purpose the *parallel group technique* was used. This involved pretesting children on a number of skills or concepts in a given curriculum area and equating them into two groups on the basis of pretest scores. One group would be designated as the *active game group* (experimental group) and an attempt made to develop the skills or concepts through the active game medium. The other group would be designated as the *traditional group* (control group) and an attempt made to develop the skills or concepts through one or more traditional media. Both groups were taught by the same teacher over a specified period of time. At the end of the experiment both groups would be retested and comparisons made of the first and second test scores of each group and the second test scores of both groups.

Along with the above standard procedure, a number of variations of this technique have been employed. In studying the effectiveness of the active game learning medium for boys compared to girls, a procedure was used that involved parallel groups of boys and girls within the total single group.

In a variation in which an attempt was made to hold the motivational variable constant, three groups were used. One group was involved in active games, a second group observed the first group without participating, and a third group was taught through traditional media.

Another variation has been to equate children into two groups, with each group taught by a different teacher. The purpose of this has been to compare the physical education teacher, who would not likely be skilled in teaching concepts in another academic area, with a superior classroom teacher who would be likely to be highly skilled in this direction.

In all of these studies the experiment is usually carried on over a period of ten days. There are ordinarily eight and sometimes as many as ten skills or concepts involved. A ten-day period allows for two days of testing and eight days of teaching. Reliability for the objective tests has ordinarily been obtained by using a test-retest with similar groups of children. All of our experiments have been done in the actual school situation. We would like to carry them out over longer periods of time, but it has been impractical to do so because it usually involves some interruption in the regular school program.

SOME REPRESENTATIVE RESEARCH FINDINGS

In the first study reported here, twenty third-grade children were equated into two groups on the basis of pretest scores on ten language understandings.[1] One group was taught through the active medium. The other group was taught through tradi-

---

[1]Humphrey, James H.: Comparison of the use of active games and language workbook exercises as learning media in the development of language understandings with third grade children. *Perceptual and Motor Skills, 21:23, 1965.*

tional language workbooks. Both groups had the same teacher. Comparisons were made of the pretest and post-test scores of the langauge workbook group and also the active game group. The statistical analysis showed that both groups learned but that the active game group learned at a higher level of significance. When the post-test scores of both groups were analyzed, it was indicated that the active game group learned significantly more than the language workbook group.

In recognition of the limitations imposed by a study of this nature, it was concluded that if one accepts the significant differences in the test scores as evidence of learning, these third-grade children could develop language comprehension through both active games and the traditional language workbook medium, although the active game medium produced greater changes.

The purpose of this next study was to compare the use of physical education activities as a learning medium with traditional teaching procedures in the development of selected fifth-grade science concepts.[2] (Stunts as well as active games were used as learning activities in this study.) In this study the science concepts were equated rather than the children. The reason for this was that an experiment that involved the equating of children would have caused too much confusion in the particular school situation where the experiment was carried out.

Seventy-two science concepts on a fifth-grade level were collected and compiled into a rating scale. These concepts were rated by a jury for difficulty of development with an average fifth-grade class. The jury consisted of five superior fifth-grade teachers and five other educators in administrative or supervisory capacities. The eighteen concepts rated as the most difficult to develop with an average fifth-grade class were selected for use in this study.

Nine physical education activities were selected to use as learning activities for developing nine of the eighteen science concepts. Traditional procedures were used to teach the remaining nine

[2]Ison, Charles F.: An experimental study of a comparison of the use of physical education activities as a learning medium with traditional teaching procedures in the development of selected fifth grade science concepts. Master's thesis, University of Maryland, College Park, Maryland, 1961.

concepts. The eighteen science concepts were taught in this manner by two fifth-grade teachers in separate schools. One science period was used to teach each concept, and the two methods by which the concepts were developed were alternated. No significant difference was found between the post-test scores of the concepts that were taught through the different methods. Significant differences were found at a high level of confidence in both classes between pretest and post-test scores of the concepts taught through the physical education medium. This condition existed in only one of the classes taught through traditional procedures. However, it could only be concluded that both procedures provided valid learning experiences with these particular concepts. A factor strongly favoring the physical education medium was that the classroom teachers' preparation and experience had been with the traditional procedures rather than with the physical education medium.

A follow-up of the study just reported was conducted by equating children rather than concepts.[3] A large number of fifth-grade pupils were pretested, and on the basis of the test results, forty-eight of them were equated into two groups of matched pairs. One group was designated as the physical education group and the other as the traditional group. The same teacher taught both groups the nine concepts. The traditional group was taught through such procedures as oral presentation, visual aids, class discussion, and experimentation. The physical education group was taught through physical education activities in which the concepts were inherent. After instruction of both groups over a nine-day period, they were retested. Comparisons of the post-tests of both groups showed a statistically significant difference in mean scores in favor of the physical education group. In this study it could be concluded that learning took place better through the physical education medium than through the traditional procedures.

This next study is an example of the single group experimental procedure with parallel groups of boys and girls within the single group.[4] The purpose of this study was to determine how well a

    3Humphrey, James H.: *Child Learning Through Elementary School Physical Education*. Dubuque, Iowa, Wm. C. Brown Co., 1966.

group of first-grade children might develop number concepts through the active game medium and at the same time to ascertain whether the approach was more favorable for boys or for girls.

Thirty-five first-grade children were pretested on eight number concepts which were to be included as a part of their regular class work during the ensuing two weeks. Ten boys and ten girls who had the same test scores as the boys were selected for the experiment. Eight active games in which the number concepts were involved and which were appropriate for use at first-grade level were selected.

The active games were taught to the twenty children and used as learning media for the development of number concepts. They were retested after the active game medium was used. The scores of the first test for all of the twenty children ranged from 30 to 73 and the scores on the second test from 59 to 78. The mean score of the first test was 51.7, and the mean score of the second test was 68. In computing the results for the ten boys and ten girls separately, the mean score for the second test for the boys was 70.5 and for the girls, 65.5. The statistical analysis showed that as a total single group, there was a highly signficant difference from pretest to post-test mean scores. In comparing boys with girls, the results indicated greater changes in learning were produced with the boys.

For a clearer picture of the direction of differences between the boys and girls, the percentages of differences in gain on a paired per pupil basis follow:

Subject Pair	Differences in % of Gain	Sex
1	0	
2	11	Boy
3	0	
4	8	Girl
5	41	Boy
6	40	Boy
7	31	Boy
8	34	Boy
9	64	Boy
10	28	Girl

[4]Humphrey, James H.: An exploratory study of active games in learning of number concepts by first grade boys and girls. *Perceptual and Motor Skills, 23:* 1966.

Six of the boys had a greater percentage difference in gain than the girls, while two of the girls had a greater percentage difference in gain. In two cases there was no difference.

In the next study presented here the parallel group experimental procedures was used.[5] The purpose was to determine how well second-grade children could learn certain number processes through traditional procedures compared to learning the same processes through what we call *active game-oriented reading content*. In the area of mathematics we refer to this kind of reading content as a *mathematics motor activity story*.[6]

The purpose of the mathematics motor activity story is to put into story form an active game in which one or more mathematics concepts are inherent. The development of such a story involves selecting an active game suitable for a particular age level and in which certain mathematics understandings may be inherent. A story is then composed from the game and written to the readability level for a given grade. An example of such a story follows. The name of this story is "Come with Me." The readability of this example is 1.5, which means fifth month of first grade. The mathematics concepts and learnings inherent in the story are rational counting, addition, and subtraction.

Come With Me

Children stand close together in a ring. One child is "it!" "It" goes around the ring. "It" will tap a child. "It" will say, "Come with me." That child will follow "It." "It" will say, "Go Home!" All run to a place in the ring. "It" will try to get a place. One child does not get a place. Now he is "It." Tell how many were tapped. Tell how many were not tapped. Play again.[7]

Two groups of second-grade children with twenty-one in one group and twenty-three in the other group were pretested on two-

---

[5]Humphrey, James H.: Comparison of the use of the physical education learning medium with traditional procedures in the development of certain arithmetical processes with second grade children. *Research Abstracts*, Washington, D. C. American Association for Health, Physical Education, and Recreation, 1968.

[6]Humphrey, James H.: The mathematics motor activity story. *The Arithmetic Teacher, 14*:14, 1967.

[7]Humphrey, James H.: Teaching children mathematics through games, stunts and rhythms, (Teacher's guide for Kimbo LP No. 5000). Deal, New Jersey, Kimbo Educational Records, 1968, p. 15.

number addition facts, three-number addition equations, and sub-traction facts. One group of children, designated as the experimental group, was taught through six mathematics motor activity stories of the type illustrated above. The other group, designated as the control group, was taught through such traditional procedures as the printed number line, plastic discs, and abstract algorithms. The experiment was conducted over a four-day period, and both groups were taught by the same teacher. At the end of the four-day period both groups having been taught the processes as indicated above were retested with the same test. At an extended interval of ten days after the post-test, the same test was given again with the same statistical procedures applied to the post-test and extended interval test. The gain from pretest to post-test favored the experimental group, and essentially the same results were obtained in gain from post-test to extended interval test. It was concluded from the results of this study that these second-grade children could develop certain number processes better and perhaps retain them longer through the active game learning medium than through some of the traditional procedures.

It seems pertinent to mention certain observations made during this study that could not show up in the statistical analysis. It was noted that the children in the experimental group appeared to be stimulated by the use of the active game learning medium. In fact, some of them commented, "We didn't have arithmetic today." This could mean that the learning activities were enjoyed to the extent that the children might not have been aware of the particular number skills they were using. It should be mentioned in connection with this study that the teacher did not attempt to relate any of the active games to the learning situation. This was done purposely in order to see how well the children would do without specific application of the active games being made in the development of a particular concept. However, as mentioned in Chapter Two, such application should ordinarily be made, as would be the case in any good teaching-learning situation.

In a study designed to evaluate the effectiveness of active games as a means of reinforcng reading skills with fourth-grade children, the parallel experimental procedure was employed.[8] The purpose of this study was to determine how well certain reading skills could be reinforced by the active game medium as compared with some of the traditional ways of reinforcing these skills.

Seventy-three fourth-grade children were pretested on eight reading skills. Thirty of these children were divided into two groups on a matched-pair basis. One group of fifteen was designated as the active games group and the other group of fifteen as the traditional group. Each reading skill was introduced and presented verbally to the two groups together. The groups were then separated, and with one group the reading skills were reinforced through various forms of active games. With the other group the reading skills were reinforced by such traditional media as a language workbook, dictionary, and prepared ditto sheets. Both groups were taught by the same teacher. The types of reading skills used in the study were structural analysis, phonics, word recognition, and vocabulary development.

After the reading skills were presented in the manner described, both groups were retested. The experiment covered ten school days, allowing one day for pretesting, eight days for the experiment, and a final day for post-testing. In fourteen of the fifteen matched pairs, the child in the active game group scored higher on the post-test than did his counterpart in the traditional group. A comparison of the post-test mean scores showed that the active game group learned significantly more than the traditional group. Therefore, it was concluded that the kinds of reading skills used in this study could be reinforced to better advantage by the active game learning medium than by some traditional approaches.

This next study also involved reinforcement of learning through physical activities.[9] (Stunts and rhythms as well as active games were used as learning activities in this study.)

8Humphrey, James H.: The use of the active game learning medium in the reinforcement of reading skills with fourth grade children. *The Journal of Special Education*, 1:369, 1967.

9Prager, Iris J.: The use of physical education activities in the reinforcement of selected first-grade science concepts. Master's thesis, University of Maryland, College Park, Maryland, 1968.

Twenty-three first-grade children were pretested on a science unit on simple machines. The children were equated into two groups on the basis of the pretest. The classroom teacher taught eight science lessons to the entire class of twenty-three children to illustrate eight first-grade science concepts involving simple machines. The teacher used regular traditional teaching procedures with the class.

Immediately after each science lesson the physical education teacher took eleven of the children (experimental group) on the basis of the pretest scores and attempted to reinforce the concepts through various kinds of physical education activities. The other twelve children (control group) took part in pleasurable activities such as artwork or story telling with the classroom teacher. These activities with the control group were not related to the science concepts.

After the procedure was followed for a two-week period, all of the children were retested. The result of this post-test showed that the group whose learning was reinforced by the physical education medium was significantly greater than the group not reinforced by physical education learning activities. In comparing each group separately as its own control, it was indicated that the group reinforced by the physical education learning activities gained significantly at a very high level of probability, while the other group did not improve significantly. The results also showed that the reinforcement procedure was more favorable for boys than for girls at this age level.

On the basis of the results of this study, the following conclusions appeared warranted:

1. The use of physical education activities should be considered as a reinforcement aid in teaching first-grade science concepts.

2. This procedure should be considered in developing science concepts with first-grade boys because the results were so favorable to learning for boys.

3. The physical education teacher might well be considered an important consultant in the planning of certain types of learning experiences in the science curriculum.

In the next study reported here, a large number of pupils were involved in a comparison of the active game learning medium with two other procedures in developing concepts related to the telling of time.[10]

Forty-two classes of third-grade pupils, for a total of 1,147 children, from eighteen school districts were used as subjects in this study. The original parent population from which the 42 classes were randomly selected consisted of 319 third-grade classes from 166 elementary schools.

The forty-two classes were divided into three groups of fourteen each. One group was taught through the developmental-meaningful method. A second group was taught through the drill method, and with the third group the active game approach was used. All classes were taught by their own classroom teacher.

Three sets of lesson plans, one for each group, were devised. Instructions to the teachers were included in each set of lesson plans. Lesson plans for the developmental-meaningful group closely followed the objectives, suggested activities, and problems used in the several textbooks most prevalent in the area. Lesson plans for the drill group and active game group paralleled the materials covered in the developmental-meaningful group. In the lesson plans for the drill group, the suggestions took the form of having the pupils work prepared examples in individual drill booklets. In the lesson plans for the active game group, the suggestions took the form of pleasurable active games. A twelve-foot clock was painted on the playground of each school using the active game procedure, and materials needed for the implementation of the program were made available. Included in this equipment were four playground balls, two sets of flash cards, and one set of numbered blocks.

There were ten teaching days in the experiment. All teachers were required to teach each lesson in twenty-minute periods. A lesson began immediately after the teacher had read the stated objectives for the current lesson. All teachers taught the time-

---

[10]Crist, Thomas: A comparison of the use of the active game learning medium with developmental-meaningful and drill procedures in developing concepts for telling time at third grade level. Doctoral Dissertation, University of Maryland, College Park, Maryland, 1968.

telling lesson at the same time each day. Teachers who used the active game approach considered time spent on lesson plans for this experiment as part of their arithmetic class rather than part of their physical education time.

Two parallel forms (Forms A and B) of a performance test in time-telling concepts were constructed and used as criterion measures for the study. Each form of the criterion measure contained seventy-four items divided into two main parts. Part I of each form consisted of sixty items purported to measure primarily a basic understanding of time telling and the comprehension of the passing time. Part II of each form consisted of fourteen verbal problems. Form A was administered as a pretest and form B was administered as a post-test.

In comparing the pretest and post-test of each individual group as its own control, it was indicated that all groups learned significantly from pretest to post-test. However, the highest level of probability was shown in the active game group, the second highest in the developmental-meaningful group, followed by the drill group. When a comparison was made of the post-test scores of all three groups, there was no significant difference between any of the three groups.

In view of the fact that none of the teachers taking part in the experiment had ever taught an academic concept using the active game technique, it seemed reasonable to consider that any conclusions drawn from the results must necessarily take this factor into consideration. It was also necessary to assume that all of the teachers had some, if not considerable, preparation and experience in the use of the developmental-meaningful and drill teaching procedures. Therefore, it would appear justifiable to speculate what results would be obtained if a similar experiment could be carried out using teachers with a physical education teacher-preparation background to teach time telling on the playground instead of teachers with general elementary education background. And further, because paper-and-pencil tests were used, the whole experimental testing procedure was slanted toward the two tradiional classroom procedures. Again, one could speculate as to the results if the testing (post-test) had been administered under one of the following circumstances: (a) testing the pupils in all three procedures in an active game locale, (b) testing the pupils taught by the active game procedure with a paper-and-pencil test and testing pupils taught by the developmental-meaningful and drill procedures in an active game media, and (c) testing pupils taught by the active game technique in an active game locale and testing pupils taught by the other two procedures with a paper-and-pencil test.

SOME GENERALIZATIONS OF THE RESEARCH FINDINGS

In view of the fact that there are now some objective data to support a long-held hypothetical postulation, perhaps some generalized assumptions along with some reasonable speculations can be set forth with some degree of confidence. Obviously, the available data reported in the foregoing studies are not extensive enough to carve out a clear-cut profile with regard to learning through active games. However, they are suggestive enough to give rise to some interesting generalizations, which may be briefly summarized as follows:

1. In general, children tend to learn certain academic skills and concepts better through the active game medium than through many of the traditional media in such subject areas as reading, science, and mathematics.

2. This approach, while favorable for both boys and girls, appears to be more favorable for boys.

3. The approach appears to be more favorable for children with normal and below normal intelligence. *Herein, lies its great value as a learning medium for slow learners.*

4. For children with high levels of intelligence, it may be possible to introduce more advanced academic skills and concepts at an earlier age through the active game learning medium.

Chapter Four

Factors Influencing Learning Through Active Games

During the early school years and at ages six to eight particularly. it is possible that learning is limited frequently by a relatively short attention span rather than only by intellectual capabilities. Moreover, some children, especially slower learners, who do not appear to think or learn well in abstract terms can more readily grasp concepts when given an opportunity to use them in an applied manner. In view of the fact that the young child lives in a *movement world,* so to speak, and also that he is likely to deal better in concrete rather than abstract terms, it would seem to follow naturally that the active game learning medium is best suited for him.

The above statement should not be interpreted to mean that the authors are suggesting that learning through movement-oriented experiences (motor learning) and passive learning experiences (verbal learning) are two different kinds of learning. The position is taken here that *learning is learning,* even though in the active game approach the motor component may be operating at a higher level than in most of the traditional types of learning activities.

The theory of learning accepted here is that learning takes place in terms of reorganization of the systems of perception into a functional and integrated whole because of the result of certain stimuli. This implies that problem solving is the way of human learning and that learning takes place through problem solving. In an active game learning situation that is well planned, a great deal of consideration will be given to the inherent possibilities for learning in terms of problem solving. In fact, in most active games, opportunities abound for near-ideal teaching-learning situations

41

because there are many problems to be solved. The following sample questions asked by children indicate that there is a great opportunity for reflective thinking, use of judgment, and problem solving in the active game experience.

1. Why didn't I get to touch the ball more often?
2. How can we make it a better game?
3. Would two circles be better than one?
4. What were some of the things you like about the game?
5. How can I learn to throw the ball better?

Another very important factor to consider with respect to the nature of learning in active games is that a considerable part of the learnings of young children are motor in character, with the child devoting a good proportion of his attention to skills of a locomotor nature. Furthermore, learnings of a motor nature tend to usurp a large amount of the young child's time and energy and are often closely associated with other learnings. In addition, it is well known by experienced classroom teachers at the primary-grade levels that the child's motor mechanism is active to the extent that it is almost an impossibility for him to remain for a very long time in a quiet state regardless of the passiveness of the learning situation.

To demand prolonged sedentary states of young children is actually, in a sense, in defiance of a basic physiological principle. This is concerned directly with the child's basal metabolism. The term *metabolism* is concerned with physical and chemical changes in the body which involve producing and consuming energy. The rate at which these physical and chemical processes are carried on when the individual is in a state of rest represents his *basal metabolism*. Thus, the basal metabolic rate is indicative of the speed at which body fuel is changed to energy, as well as how fast this energy is used.

Basal metabolic rate can be measured in terms of calories per meter of body surface, with a calorie representing a unit measure of heat energy in food. It has been found that on the average, basal metabolism rises from birth to about two or three years of age, at which time it starts to decline until between the ages of twenty to twenty-four. Also, the rate is higher for boys than for girls. With the highest metabolic rate and therefore the greatest amount of energy occurring during the early school years, deep consideration might well be given to learning activities through which this energy can be utilized. Moreover, it has been observed that there is an increased attention span of primary-age children during play. When a task such as an active game is meaningful to a child, he can spend longer periods engaged in it than is likely to be the case in some of the more traditional types of learning activities.

The comments made thus far have alluded to some of the general aspects of the value of the active game learning medium. The ensuing discussions will focus more specifically upon what we call certain *inherent facilitative factors* in active games which are highly compatible with child learning. These factors are *motivation, proprioception,* and *reinforcement,* all of which are somewhat interdependent and interrelated.

MOTIVATION

In considering motivation as an inherent facilitative factor of learning in the active game approach, we would like to think of the term in the same manner as it is described in the *Dictionary of Education:*

> . . . the practical art of applying incentives and arousing interest for the purpose of causing a pupil to perform in a desired way; usually designates the act of choosing study materials of such a sort and presenting them in such a way that they appeal to the pupils interests and cause him to attack the work at hand willingly and to complete it with sustained enthusiasm; also designates the use of various devices such as the offering of rewards or an appeal to the desire to excel.[1]

We need also take in to account *extrinsic* and *intrinsic* motivation. Extrinsic motivation is described as "the application of incentives that are external to a given activity to make work palatable and to facilitate performance, for example, offering a prize to the pupil who makes the highest score in a spelling test as an appeal to the extrinsic desire to excel." Intrinsic motivation is the "de-

[1]Good, Carter V.: *Dictionary of Education,* 2nd ed. New York, McGraw-Hill, Inc., 1959, p. 354.

termination of behavior that is resident within an activity and that sustains it, as with autonomous acts and interests."[2]

Extrinsic motivation has been and continues to be used as a means of spurring individuals to achievement. This most often takes the form of various kinds of reward incentives. The main objection to this type of motivation is that it tends to focus the learner's attention upon the reward rather than the learning task and the total learning situation.

In general, the child is motivated when he discovers what seems to him to be a suitable reason for engaging in a certain activity. The most valid reason of course is that he sees a purpose for the activity and derives enjoyment from it. The child must feel that what he is doing is important and purposeful. When this occurs and the child gets the impression that he is being successful in a group situation, the motivation is intrinsic, since it comes about naturally as a result of the child's interest in the activity. It is the premise here that the active game approach contains this "built-in" ingredient so necessary to desirable and worthwhile learning.

The ensuing discussions of this section of the chapter will be concerned with three aspects of motivation that are considered to be inherent in the active game learning medium. These are (a) motivation in relation to *interest,* (b) motivation in relation to *knowledge of results,* and (c) motivation in relation to *competition.*

Motivation in Relation to Interest

It is important to have an understanding of the meaning of interest as well as an appreciation of how interests function as an adjunct to learning. As far as the meaning of the term is concerned, the following description given some time ago by Lee and Lee expresses in a relatively simple manner what is meant by the terms *interest* and *interests:* "*Interest* is a state of being, a way of reacting to a certain situation. *Interests* are those fields or areas to which a child reacts with interest consistently over an extended period of time."[3]

---

[2]*Ibid.*

[3]Lee, J. Murray, and Lee, Dorris May: *The Child and His Development.* New York, Appleton-Century-Crofts, 1958, p. 382.

There is a principle of learning that suggests that "learning takes place best when the child agrees with and acts upon the learnings which he considers of most value to him."[4] This means that the child accepts as most valuable those things that are of greatest interest to him. To the very large majority of children, their active play experiences are of the greatest personal value to them.

Under most circumstances a very high interest level is concomitant with active game situations simply because of the expectation of pleasure children tend to associate with such activities. The structure of a learning activity is directly related to the length of time the learning act can be tolerated by the learner without loss of interest. Active game situations by their very nature are more likely to be so structured than many of the traditional learning activities.

Motivation in Relation to Knowledge of Results

Knowledge of results is most commonly referred to as *feedback*. It was suggested by Brown many years ago that feedback is the process of providing the learner with information as to how accurate his reactions were.[5] Ammons has referred to feedback as knowledge of various kinds which the performer received about his performance.[6]

It has been reported by Bilodeau and Bilodeau that knowledge of results is the strongest, most important variable controlling performance and learning, and further that studies have repeatedly shown that there is no improvement without it, progressive improvement with it, and deterioration after its withdrawal.[7] As a matter of fact, there appears to be a sufficient abundance of

---

[4]Humphrey, James H.: *Child Learning Through Elementary School Physical Education.* Dubuque, Iowa, Wm. C. Brown Co., 1966, p. 109.

[5]Brown, J. S.: A proposed program of research on psychological feedback (knowledge of results) in the performance of psychomotor tasks. Research Planning Conference on Perceptual and Motor Skills, AFHRRC Conf. Rept. 1949, U. S. Air Force, San Antonio, Texas, pp. 1-98.

[6]Ammons, R. B.: Effects of knowledge of performance: A survey and tentative theoretical formulation. *Journal of General Psychology, LIV:* 279-99, 1956.

[7]Bilodeau, Edward A., and Bilodeau, Ina: Motor skill learning. *Annual Review of Psychology,* Palo Alto, Calif., 1961, pp. 243-70.

objective evidence that indicates that learning is usually more effective when one receives some immediate information on how he is progressing. It would appear rather obvious that such knowledge of results is an important adjunct to learning because one would have little idea of which of his responses were correct. Dolinsky makes the analogy that it would be like trying to learn a task while blindfolded.[8]

The active game approach to learning provides almost instantaneous knowledge of results because the child can actually *see* and *feel* himself throw a ball, or tag, or be tagged in a game. He does not become the victim of a poorly constructed paper-and-pencil test, the results of which may have little or no meaning for him. This is particularly important as far as the slower learning child is concerned.

Motivation in Relation to Competition

In discussing competition as a factor of motivation, it might be well to repeat our description of active games that appeared in Chapter Two. That is, active games imply *active interaction of children in cooperative and/or competitive situations.* It is possible to have both cooperation and competition functioning at the same time, as in the case of team games. While one team is competing against the other, there is cooperation within each group. It is also possible to have one group competing against another without cooperation within the groups. An example of this type of game is Steal the Bacon described previously.

It is interesting to note that the terms *cooperation* and *competition* are antonymous; therefore, the reconciliation of children's competitive needs and cooperative needs is not an easy matter. In a sense, we are confronted with an ambivalent condition, which if not carefully handled could place children in a state of conflict. Horney recognized this many years ago when she stated:

> On the one hand everything is done to spur us toward success, which means that we must be not only assertive but aggressive, able to push others out of the way. On the other hand we are deeply imbued with Christian ideals which declare that it is

---

8Dolinsky, Richard: *Human Learning.* Dubuque, Iowa, Wm. C. Brown Co., 1966, p. 13.

selfish to want anything for ourselves, that we should be humble, turn the other hand, be yielding.[9]

Thus, modern society not only rewards one kind of behavior (competition) but also its direct opposite (cooperation). Perhaps more often than not our cultural demands sanction these rewards without provision of clear-cut standards of value with regard to specific conditions under which these forms of behavior might well be practiced. Hence, the child is placed in somewhat of a quandary with reference to when to compete and when to cooperate.

In generalizing on the basis of the available evidence with regard to the subject of competition, it appears justifiable to formuate the following concepts:

1. Very young children in general are not very competitive but become more so as they get older.

2. There is a wide variation in competition among children; that is, some are violently competitive while others are mildly competitive, and still others are not competitive at all.

3. Boys tend to be more competitive than girls.

4. Competition should be adjusted so that there is not a preponderant number of winners over losers.

5. Competition and rivalry produce results in effort and speed of accomplishment.

In the school situation teachers might well be guided by the above concepts. As far as active games are concerned, they not only appear to be a good medium for learning because of the intrinsic motivation inherent in them but also this medium of learning can provide for competitive needs of children in a pleasurable and enjoyable way.

PROPRIOCEPTION

At the outset of this chapter it was stated that the theory of learning accepted here is that learning takes place in terms of a reorganization of the systems of perception into a functional and integrated whole as a result of certain stimuli. These systems of perception, or sensory processes as they are sometimes referred to, are ordinarily considered to consist of the senses of sight, hearing,

---

[9]Horney, Karen: *The Neurotic Personality of Our Time.* New York, Norton, 1937.

touch, smell, and taste. Armington has suggested that "although this point of view is convenient for some purposes, it greatly over-simplifies the ways by which information can be fed into the human organism."[10] He indicates also that a number of sources of sensory input are overlooked, particularly the senses that enable the body to maintain its correct posture. As a matter of fact, the sixty to seventy pounds of muscle which include over six hundred in number that are attached to the skeleton of the averaged-sized man could well be his most important sense organ.

Various estimates indicate that the visual sense brings us upwards of three-fourths of our knowledge. Therefore, it could be said with little reservation that man is eye-minded. However, Steinhaus has reported that "a larger portion of the nervous system is devoted to receiving and integrating sensory input originating in the muscles and joint structures than is devoted to the eye and ear combined."[11] In view of this Steinhaus also contends that man is *muscle sense* minded.

Generally speaking, *proprioception* is concerned with muscle sense. The proprioceptors are sensory nerve terminals that give information concerning movements and position of the body. A proprioceptive feedback mechanism is involved which in a sense regulates movement. In view of the fact that children are so movement oriented, it appears a reasonable speculation that proprioceptive feedback from the receptors of muscles, skin, and joints contributes in a facilitative manner when the active game learning medium is used to develop academic skills and concepts. The combination of the psychological factor of motivation and the physiological factor of proprioception inherent in the active game approach to learning has caused us to coin the term moto*r*vation to describe this phenomenon.

If there is any credence in the old Chinese proverb that "one picture is worth a thousand words," perhaps in modern times we might wish to give consideration to the possibility of *muscle use* for learning as being worth a thousand pictures.

10Armington, John C.: *Physiological Basis of Psychology.* Dubuque, Iowa, Wm. C. Brown Co., 1966, p. 16.

11Steinhaus, Arthur H: Your muscles see more than your eyes. *Journal of Health-Physical Education-Recreation, 37*:38, Sept. 1966.

REINFORCEMENT

In considering the compatibility of the active game learning medium with reinforcement theory, the meaning of reinforcement needs to be taken into account. An acceptable general description of reinforcement would be that there is an increase in the efficiency of a response to a stimulus brought about by the concurrent action of another stimulus. The basis for contending that the active game learning medium is consistent with *general* reinforcement theory is that this medium reinforces attention to the learning task and learning behavior. It keeps children involved in the learning activity, which is perhaps the major area of application for reinforcement procedures. Moreover, there is perhaps little in the way of human behavior that is not reinforced, or at least reinforcible, by feedback of some sort, and the importance of proprioceptive feedback has already been discussed in this particular connection.

With regard to the studies mentioned in Chapter Three, the extent to which the active game learning medium is consistent with any *specific* principle of reinforcement depends upon how one interprets the data. As an example of this we allude to Premack's *specific* reinforcement hypothesis.[12] This theory suggests that an essential condition of reinforcement is a rate differential between two responses in a situation where emitting the stronger behavior is made contingent upon the prior occurrence of the weaker behavior. Stated in another way, if behavior B is of higher probability than behavior A, then behavior A can be made more probable by making behavior B contingent upon it. There could be a suggestive relation between the data presented in the preceding chapter and Premack's reinforcement hypothesis. However, to make it more than suggestive would no doubt require some independent measures of the probabilities; that is, durations for which the various subjects engaged in the designated active game learning activities in relation to those engaging in the traditional learning activities.[13]

---

[12]Premack, David: Toward empirical behavior laws: I. Positive reinforcement. *Psychological Review*, *66*:4, 1959.

[13]Premack, David: Personal communication, July 5, 1966.

In summarizing this discussion, it would appear that the active game learning medium generally establishes a more effective situation for learning reinforcement for the following reason: First, the greater motivation of the children in the active game learning situation involves accentuation of those behaviors directly pertinent to their learning activities, making these salient for the purpose of reinforcement. Second, the proprioceptive emphasis in active game learning involves a greater number of *responses* associated with and conditioned to learning stimuli. And finally, the gratifying aspects of the active game situations provide a generalized situation of *reinforcers*.

Chapter Five

Teaching Slow Learners To Read Through Active Games

The theory that there is a degree of relationship between active play and reading is not new. For example, well over two centuries ago Fenelon (1651-1715) is reputed to have said that he had seen certain children who learned to read while playing.[1] A representative statement of more modern times, and in a more specific vein, suggests that with children "the kinesthetic sense—the sense of 'feel' they get through their muscles—seems to be highly developed and it helps some children remember words they would take much longer to learn by looking at or sounding out."[2]

The following is a summary of the active games along with the inherent reading skills or language arts concepts which are explained in detail in the ensuing section of the chapter. The games have been grouped by the major aspects of the reading program. Some of the games are particularly useful for developing specific language or reading concepts. In these games the learner acts out the concept and thus is able to visualize as well as get the *feel* of the concept. Other games help to develop skills by using these skills in highly interesting and stimulating situations. The *application* section for each game indicates the appropriate use of these activities, whether for development of a concept or for skill mastery. Suggestions for adapting many of the games are made in order to extend these types of activities to other elements of the various aspects of the reading program. The games included have much versatility, depending on the creativeness of teachers.

---

[1]Johnson, George Ellsworth: *Education by Plays and Games,* Boston, Ginn and Company, 1907, p. 31.

[2]Beaumont, Florence, and Franklin, Adele: Who says Johnny can't read? *Parents Magazine,* June, 1955.

In selecting games for inclusion in Chapters Five, Six, and Seven, a set of criteria was used by the authors. The first guideline for selection was the definition of active games as discussed earlier in Chapter Two. Active games are those in which there is active interaction of children in cooperative and/or competitive situations.

A second basis for selection was the appropriateness of the game either for the development of a concept or for providing repetitive drill for development of skills related to specific concepts. Some of the games have specific concepts inherent in the activity itself. Others provide interesting and stimulating settings for developing skills through practice and repetition of these skills.

A third factor influencing choice of games for this volume was that of the complexity of the tasks involved in the game. Some games are simply too complicated in terms of rules to appeal to any but the more able learner. Those games selected were obvious enough in the inherent concept to be developed and simple enough that most children could participate in the game with enjoyment under proper guidance by the teacher.

In working with the active game approach, several guidelines can be useful to the teacher in order to provide meaningful and satisfying experiences for children. Often, games can be set up with the entire class participating. In such cases it is important that the less able learner not be penalized for his slowness or inability to perform a given task by being eliminated from the game. The games that have been selected have established procedures whereby the slow learner who needs the additional practice remains in the game and yet need not hamper the rest of the children in their competitive efforts to win. The slow learner can also be helped by the more able learners in his group.

In those games in which the children are divided into teams, it is considered a wise practice for the teacher to arrange the selection method so that there is a balance of able learners as well as the less able learners assigned to each team. This should also be considered when different physical skills are called for in a specific game. Such arranging by the teacher need not appear obvious and does help to provide a satisfying experience for all the children with a more even competition.

The teacher may also elect to use a game for one particular group of children. This is appropriate when only one group within the class needs additional work with a given skill, and to include all children would make the less able children feel inadequate and bore those children who have mastered the skill.

After a game has been played, it should be evaluated not only in terms of children's reaction to the game and how it was played but also in terms of how well the children understand the concepts inherent in the game, regardless of whether the focus is reading and the language arts, mathematics, or science. The game situation can also serve as a means of evaluating specific skill needs of children in terms of planning further instruction.

The following illustration describes an active game a teacher used to help in the development of hearing and identifying syllables in words. There had been some previous work with syllabication. This activity was used to provide practice in recognizing one-syllable and two-syllable words. During and following the activity the teacher utilized various aspects of the situation to relate the activity to the concept of syllabication and help children to see this relationship. The teacher's evaluation included the children's reaction to the game, how well they played the game, and whether they developed the skill of hearing syllables in words from the game.

Concept: Syllabication
Activity: The Ocean Is Stormy

Before going out to the activity area, the children should select the names of approximately six to ten fish having one-syllable names and six to ten fish have two-syllable names, depending on the size of the group. These names are written on the board, and the children are asked to remember them. The children are then divided into couples and proceed to the playing area. They group themselves by couples in the playing area, and circles are drawn in chalk around each couple except one. This extra couple is known as the Homeless Whales. The couples in the circles secretly select a name for themselves from the one-syllable fish names that had been written on the blackboard. The Homeless Whales, holding hands, walk around the playing area and call out the name of a one-syllable fish. If their fish name is called, couples leave their circles, holds hands, and fall in line behind the whales. All couples named must follow the Whales until the Whales suddenly call "The ocean is stormy." At this, all the couples trailing the Whales, and the Whales, run to an empty circle. The pair left without a circle become the Whales for the next game, and the former Whales choose a fish name. At any point in the game the teacher may suddenly call "Typhoon" whereupon everyone, including those still standing in a circle, must seek a different circle. The next time the game is played, children takes names of fish with two syllables. Later they may use three-syllable fish names. Children may have to use the encyclopedia to find fish with two or three syllables in their names.

Teaching Procedure:

Teacher: Boys and girls, do you remember the other day we were studying about different kinds of animals? What are some of the kinds of animals that we learned about? (Children.) Yes, one of the groups was fish. What were some of the characteristics of fish that we discussed? (Children.) It was interesting to find out about some of the characteristics of fish. What are some of the names of the fish we read and talked about? (Children name fish, and the teacher writes the names on the blackboard.) The other day we were finding out that words are divided into syllables. What did we say a syllable was? (Children.) Yes, they are parts of a word. Dividing a word into syllables helps us to do what? (Children.) Good. It is an aid to pronunciation, spelling, and meaning. Let's look at the names of the fish we were just talking about and see if we can hear the parts of their names and divide them into syllables. (The children read the name of each fish on the list and decide how many syllables each one has.) Let's group the one-syllable fish names together. Tell me which ones belong in this list. (The teacher writes the names the children give.) Which names belong in a list for two-syllable fish names? (Children respond, and teacher writes list.) Very good. Now let's say them once more so we will be able to remember them.

Today we are going to play a game called The Ocean Is Stormy. We are going to need to remember some of the one-syllable and two-syllable fish names in order to play our game. (The teacher goes over the procedures and answers any questions the children may have. The children move to the playing area and proceed with the game. During the game the teacher may make comments.) Whales, make sure that you say the names of the fish loud enough so we can all hear you. You can also do things besides walk. You may run, skip, jump, or anything you choose. Whatever you do, the rest of the fish must follow. All right. Let's continue. (Children play game.)

The activity continues for a time, and then the teacher evaluates with the class.

Teacher: Did you like The Ocean Is Stormy? (Children.) Are you better able to remember the names of the fish? (Children.) Are you better able to hear the number of syllables in the names of the fish? (Children.) Do you think the game helped you to hear syllables in words? (Children.) How can we improve our playing of The Ocean Is Stormy? (Children.)

CLASSIFICATION OF GAMES ACCORDING TO MAJOR AREAS IN READING

The following is a summary of the active games that contain reading and language arts concepts and skills. Descriptions of the games follow the summary.

Concept	*Game*
Word Analysis Skills:	
Recognizing Letters of the Alphabet	Letter Snatch
	Large And Small
	Magic Vowels
Auditory Discrimination—	Match The Sound
Beginning Sounds, Consonants,	Man From Mars
Consonant Blends, Consonant	Crows And Cranes
Digraphs, Vowels	Call Blends
	Final Blend Change
	Mouse And Cheese
	Vowels In A Basket
	Build A Word

Rhyming Words	Rhyme Chase
	Add A Word
	Rhyme Grab
Initial Consonant Substitution	First Letter Change
Visual Discrimination— Whole Words	See The Same
	Cross The Bridge
Auditory and Visual Association— Initial Consonants	Consonant Relay
	Erase The Beginning
Visual Letter Patterns—Vowel Sound Principles	Letter Pattern Change
Plurals of Nouns	Plural Relay
Inflectional Endings	Ending Relay
Syllabication	Syllable Relay
	The Ocean Is Stormy
Accent	Accent Relay
Alphabetical Order	Alphabet Relay
	Alphabet Line-Up
	Jumping Rope
	Alphabet Throw
Guide Words in Dictionary	Where Is The Word
Sight Vocabulary:	
	Word Carpet (Variation)
	Call Phrase
	Word Steps
	Word Toss
	Word Erase
	Words In A Circle
	Squirrel With A Nut
Comprehension:	
Following Directions	Simon Says
	Do This, Do That

Classification	Pet Store
	Ducks Fly
Vocabulary Meaning	Match The Meaning
	Word Hunt
	Rainbow
	The Mulberry Bush
	Changing Seats
	Over And Under Relay
	Weather Bureau
	Word Action
	What To Play
	Action Relay
	Word Change
	I'm Tall, I'm Small
	Opposites Relay
Sequence of Events	Sentence Relay

Word Analysis Skills

Concept: Recognizing Letters of the Alphabet

Activity: Letter Snatch

The children are divided into two teams of eight to ten each. The teams face each other about ten to twelve feet apart. A small object such as an eraser is placed on the floor between the two teams. The members on both teams are given like letters. The teacher then holds up a card with a letter on it. The children from each team who have the letter run out and try to grab the object and return to their line. If the child does so without being tagged by the other child, he scores two points. If he is tagged, the other team scores one point.

Application:

Children have the opportunity to practice letter recognition in this activity. Visual matching can be with all small letters at first and then later with all capital letters. After the children have learned both small and capital letters, one team can have small letters and the other use capital letters, with the teacher displaying cards showing either type letter.

Concept: Recognizing Letters of the Alphabet—Matching Capital and Small Letters

Activity: Large and Small

The children are divided into two teams of eight to ten each. The teams stand in lines about fifteen feet apart and face in the same direction. The children on the first team are each given a card with a small letter on it. Each member of the second team is given a card with corresponding capital letters. The members of the first team hold their cards behind them for the second team to be able to see. The teacher touches a child on the second team. The child then runs over to the first team, finds the child with the same letter as his, and tags the child. The child on the first team turns and chases the child who tagged him, who tries to get back into place before the other child touches him. If he is tagged, the first team gets one point; if he gets back safely, team two gets one point. After each child on the second team has had an opportunity to match his letter, the teacher then gives the children on the first team the opportunity to match letters. To do this, the teams should both face in the opposite direction so that the first team can now see the letters the children on the second team hold behind their backs.

Application:

This game provides the necessary experience in associating capital and small letters that children need to become more familiar with the letters of the alphabet in upper and lower case form.

Concept: Recognizing Letters of the Alphabet—Vowels

Activity: Magic Vowels

The playing area is considered the Magic Area. The vowels marked on it represent Magic Spots. The children line up in a single file and follow a leader around the area. When a stop signal is given, all those on Magic Spots are safe and score a point if they can name the vowel they are standing on. Those who are not standing on a Magic Spot or who cannot name the vowel do not score. The child with the most points wins.

Application:

Children need opportunities to practice identification of the vowel letters. This game provides the drill to aid in the recognition of the vowel letters. Children who are having difficulty are not eliminated from the game and are thereby given the chance to continue working with the vowels until they become more familiar with them.

Concept: Auditory Discrimination—Beginning Sounds in Words
Activity: Match The Sound

A group of eight to ten children form a circle. The children skip around in the circle until the teacher gives a signal to stop. The teacher then says a word and throws a ball directly at one of the children. The teacher begins to count to ten. The child who catches the ball must say another word which begins with the same sound before the teacher counts to ten. If the child does, he gets a point. The children with the most points wins. The other children in the circle must listen carefully to be sure each child calls out a correct word. As the children learn to associate letter names with sounds, the child must not only call another word beginning with the same sound but also must identify the letter that word begins with.

Application:

This game enables children to listen for sounds in the initial position of words. The game can also be adapted to listening for final position sounds.

Concept: Auditory Discrimination—Beginning Sounds in Words
Activity: Man From Mars

One child is selected to be the Man from Mars and stands in the center of the play area. The other children stand behind a designated line at one end of the play area. The game begins when the children call out, "Man from Mars, can we chase him through the stars?" The teacher answers, "Yes, if your name begins like duck." (Or any other word). All the children whose name begin with the same beginning sound as *duck* or whatever word is called, chase the Man from Mars until he is caught. The child who tags him becomes the new Man from Mars, and the game continues.

Application:

In order for the children to run at the right time, they must listen carefully and match beginning sounds. If the teacher sees a child not running when he should, individual help can be given.

Concept: Auditory Discrimination—Consonant Blends
Activity: Crows and Cranes

The playing area is divided by a center line. On opposite ends of the area are drawn base lines, parallel to the center line. The class is divided into two teams. The children of one team are designated as Crows and take position on one side of the play area, with the base line on their side of the center line serving as their safety zone. The members of the other team are designated as Cranes and take position on the other side of the play area, with their base line as a safety zone. The teacher stands to one side of the play area by the center line. The teacher then calls out, "Cr-r-anes" or "Cr-r-ows." In calling cranes or crows, the teacher emphasizes the initial consonant blend. If the teacher calls the Crows, they turn and run to their base line to avoid being tagged. The Cranes attempt to tag their opponents before they can cross their base line. The Cranes score a point for each Crow tagged. The Crows and Cranes then return to their places, and the teacher proceeds to call one of the groups; play continues in the same manner. This game can be extended to include other words beginning with consonant blends, for example, swans and swallows, storks and starlings, squids and squabs.

Application:

Repetition of the consonant blends during the game helps children become aware of these sounds and to develop their auditory perception of the blends in the context of words. Discovering names of animals with other consonant blends can help children in their ability to hear consonant blends in the initial position of words.

Concept: Auditory Discrimination—Consonant Blends
Activity: Call Blends

Eight to ten children stand in a circle. The teacher stands in the center of the circle, holding a ball. Each child is assigned an initial consonant blend by the teacher (st, gr, bl, cl, and so forth). When the teacher calls out a word with an initial consonant blend, the ball is thrown into the air. The child assigned that blend must then call a word using the blend and catch the ball after it has bounced once. Depending on the ability level of the children, the teacher can control the amount of time between calling out the blend-word and the time the child catches the ball and calls out his word. When the child gives a correct word and catches the ball, he scores one point. The child with the most points wins. The teacher can reassign blends frequently to the children during the game.

Application:

This activity is a supplemental one to reinforce previous auditory and visual presentation of consonant blends in the initial position. Blends used in the game should be those with which the children have worked. The teacher may write the word on the board after each time and have the child underline the blend in order to reinforce the blend in the visual context of the word.

Concept: Auditory Discrimination—Final Consonant Blends
(nk, ck, nd, st, nt, rst)

Activity: Final Blend Change

The children form a single circle, with one child standing in the center of the circle. The children in the circle are designated as different final consonant blends. Several children will be assigned the same blends. Each child may be given a card with his blend written on it to help him remember. The teacher then pronounces a word with one of the final position blends. All the children with this blend must hold up their card and then run to exchange places. The child in the center tries to get to one of the vacant places in the circle. The remaining child goes to the center.

Application:

This game helps children to develop their auditory discrimination of final position blends. They must listen carefully to the words pronounced. By holding up their card, they are associating the visual with the auditory symbol for that sound. The teacher may write the word down that is called out and have one of the children underline the final consonant blend so they can see the blend in the context of the whole word.

Concept: Auditory Discrimination—Consonant Digraphs (ch, sh, th)

Activity: Mouse And Cheese

A round mousetrap is formed by the children standing in a circle. In the center of the mousetrap is placed the cheese, a ball, or some other object. The children are then assigned consonant digraphs *sh, ch,* and *th,* instead of counting off by one, two, and three. When the teacher calls a word beginning with a consonant digraph, all the children with this digraph run around the circle and back to their original place, representing the holes in the trap. Through these original places they run into the circle to get the cheese. The child who gets the cheese is the winning mouse. Another word is called, and the same procedure is followed. Children may be reassigned digraphs from time to time.

Application:

Children need repetition for developing the ability to hear and identify various sound elements within words. This game enables children to recognize consonant digraphs within the context of whole words. A variation of this game would be to have the teacher hold up word cards with words beginning with consonants digraphs rather than saying the word. This variation would provide emphasis on visual discrimination of initial consonant digraphs. Another variation would focus on ending consonant digraphs, either auditory or visual recognition.

Concept: Auditory Discrimination—Vowels

Activity: Vowels In A Basket

Eight to ten children form a circle and count off by two's. This means that alternating children in the circle are on team one while the others are on team two. The children remain in a single circle. A scorekeeper is appointed to keep score for each team. A wastebasket is placed in the center of the circle. The object of the game is for each child to give a word with a different vowel from the one in a word the teacher calls, for example *bed-bad, hip-hop, had-hid,* and then to toss the beanbag into the wastebasket. One point is scored for a correct medial-vowel substitution and another point for a successful throw. The beanbag passes around the circle with each child responding to a word and throwing the beanbag.

Each child's score must be correctly assigned to his team. All children should be encouraged to listen to be sure the children have given real words rather than nonsense words. The child who does not give a correct word remains in the game but scores no point for his team. The team with the highest score wins.

Application:

Children need practice in working with medial vowels in the context of meaningful words. The teacher can reinforce the vowels used in the words by writing each set of words on the blackboard so the children can see the vowels in context. To make the game more difficult, the teacher can also require a child to identify which vowel was in the word that was called and in the word given by the child. For children having difficulty in hearing vowel sounds, another adaptation might be to use familiar sight vocabulary words and print them on large-size cards. The teacher can then display the word and say the word at the same time.

Concept: Auditory Discrimination—Vowels

Activity: Build A Word

The children are divided into several teams. The teams stand in rows* behind a starting line about ten to fifteen feet from the blackboard. The teacher calls a word. The first child on each team runs to the board and writes another word with that vowel sound on the board. He then returns to his team and tags the next child. The second child then writes a second word with the same vowel sound on the board. If an error is made, the teacher helps the child correct it before the next child takes his turn. This procedure continues until every child has written a word on the board. The team finishing first scores a point. Another word is then called.

Application:

This game can be played when children have been introduced to vowel sounds, either a few or all of them. Words called by the teacher reflect those vowels with which the children have been working. Words can be called using only the short sounds of all the vowels, then the long sounds of all the vowels, then both long

---

*In a *file, row,* or *column* the children stand one behind the other. In a *line* the children stand beside each other shoulder to shoulder.

and short sounds of one vowel, and finally long and short sounds of all vowels. This game can be adapted to working with initial and final consonants.

Concept: Rhyming Words

Activity: Rhyme Chase

The children form a circle. Each child is given a card with a familiar word from the children's sight vocabulary written on it. The teacher may ask each child to pronounce his word before beginning the game. The children should listen and look at the words as each one identifies his word. The teacher then calls out a word that rhymes with one or several of the words held by the children. The child (or children) holds up his rhyming word so all the children can see it. He must then give another word that rhymes with his word. This is the signal for all children to run to a safety space previously designated by the teacher. The child (or children) try to tag any one of the children before he reaches a safe place. A child who is tagged receives a point. The object is for the children to get the lowest score possible. Word cards may be exchanged among the children after several turns.

Application:

In this activity the children are called upon to relate auditory experiences in rhyming with visual presentations of these words. Sight vocabulary is also emphasized as the children reinforce the concept of visual patterns in rhyming words.

Concept: Rhyming Words

Activity: Add A Word

The group is divided into several teams. The teams line up in rows behind a starting line some fifteen feet from the blackboard. On a signal the first child of each team runs to the board and writes a word with which he knows another word will rhyme. When he returns, he hands the chalk to the next child on his team. The second child then writes a word under the first word that rhymes with it. The next child continues to do the same. When a team member cannot think of a word to add to the list already given, he writes a new word that he knows will rhyme with another word. This continues until all the children have had a turn. Scoring is as shown:

First Team			Second Team	
cat	1 point		can	1 point
fat	2 points		man	2 points
rat	3 points		fan	3 points
sat	4 points		may	1 point
well	1 point		say	2 points
bell	2 points		get	1 point
tell	3 points		no	1 point
Total	16 points		*Total*	11 points

Misspelled words earn no points. To vary the game or increase vocabulary, the teacher may write the introductory or new word each time for both teams. The team with the highest score wins.

Application:

This game provides an interesting approach to reinforcing the rhyming skills of children. To make the maximum score, the children are encouraged to rhyme as many words as possible. They must also be able to distinguish between rhyming and nonrhyming words to score the game properly. The teacher might want to note types of spelling errors made for further instruction.

Concept: Rhyming Words

Activity: Rhyme Grab

The class is divided into two teams. The teams line up and face each other about fifteen to twenty feet apart. A ball or beanbag is placed in the center of the area between the two teams. The members of each team are given corresponding rhyming words. The teacher calls a word. The children who have words that rhyme with the one the teacher calls try to snatch the ball. The child who gets the ball scores a point for his team. The team with the most points wins.

Application:

Children need to have many situations that call upon their auditory skill in hearing words that rhyme. In this game children may also be given an opportunity to associate printed words with spoken words by having the teacher alternate holding up word cards and the children determining if the word assigned them rhymes with the printed word, or giving the children word cards and the teacher calling out words.

Concept: Initial Consonant Substitution

Activity: First Letter Change

The class is divided into several teams. The teams stand in rows behind a starting line some ten to fifteen feet from the blackboard. A word such as *ball* is written on the board for each team. (To prevent copying, different words should be used for each team.) On a signal the first child on each team goes to the board, says the word, writes another word, changing the initial consonant to make another meaningful word, says the word, and then runs to the rear of his team. The second child of the team repeats this same sequence. The first team to complete the writing of words with initial consonant substitution correctly scores a point. Any child having trouble may ask the help of one member of his team to identify another word.

Application:

Children are able to develop their skills in using initial consonant substitution in this activity with the added dimension of visual and kinesthetic experiences by seeing a word and writing new words, using different initial consonants.

Concept: Visual Discrimination—Whole Words

Activity: See The Same

The children are divided into two groups. Sets of word cards are made up and placed in a large, shallow box, one for each team. The words selected are those being developed as sight vocabulary. A pair of word cards is made up for each word. The words are then mixed up in the boxes. The two teams stand in rows behind a starting line. On a signal the first child of each group runs to the group's box and looks for two words that are alike. He then displays the pair of words on a sentence chart holder that is set up next to the group's box. The next child in the group proceeds in the same manner. The first group who has each child find a pair of words wins. A child having difficulty may seek the help from one member of his group.

Application:

Children need opportunities to visually match not only letters but also words in order for them to develop the skills of seeing letter elements within the gestalt of the whole word. This activity provides an interesting means for developing this skill. The teacher may encourage the children to identify the word pair they have found. (If there are additional sentence chart holders, it is desirable to have smaller groups and thus more teams.)

Concept: Visual Discrimination—Whole Words
Activity: Cross The Bridge

The play area is marked off with lines at each end. A child is selected to be the Bridge Keeper. He stands in the center of the play area while the remainder of the class stands behind one end line. Each child is given a card with a sight vocabulary word on it. Several children should have the same word. The Bridge Keeper is given a box with a complete set of word cards that correspond to those given the other children and large enough for all children to see. The children call out to the Bridge Keeper, "May we use the bridge? May we use the Bridge?" The Bridge Keeper replies, "Yes, if you are this word." He then holds up one of the word cards from his box for all the children to see. The child or children having that word try to cross to the other end line without being tagged by the Bridge Keeper. The procedure is continued again with other words. Those children tagged must help the Bridge Keeper to tag the other children as they also try to cross the bridge. Occasionally the Bridge Keeper may call out, "Everybody cross the Bridge," when all the children may then run to the opposite end line. The game can continue until one child remains. He becomes the Bridge Keeper for the next game, or another Bridge Keeper may be selected.

Application:

This activity provides children the opportunity to match words visually as a means to reinforce words to the point that they may become a part of the child's sight vocabulary.

Concept: Auditory and Visual Association—Initial Consonants
Activity: Consonant Relay

The children are divided into several relay teams. The teams line up at a specified distance from a blackboard and are seated. The teacher stands so as to be seen by the children when pronouncing the words. The teacher says a word beginning with a consonant sound. The last child in each team runs to the board, writes the beginning consonant, and returns to the head of his team. Each child moves back one place. The first child to get back to his seat with the correct letter written on the board scores a point for his team. The teacher says another word, and the game continues as above until everyone has had a turn. The team with the highest score wins.

Application:

This game gives children practice in hearing initial consonant sounds and associating them with their written symbols. This game can be adapted to working with final consonants, digraphs, blends, and long and short vowel sounds.

Concept: Auditory and Visual Association—Initial Consonants

Activity: Erase The Beginning

The class is divided into several teams, or a reading group may be divided into two teams. The teams form rows about ten to fifteen feet from a blackboard. A list of familiar sight vocabulary words beginning with different consonants are written on the board in front of each team. Each team's list includes words beginning with the same number of different initial consonants. There are more words in each list than there are team members. The first child of each team is given an eraser. The teacher calls a word. The first child on each team then goes to the board and erases one word from his list that begins with the same letter. (The teacher may repeat the word once while the children are at the board.) To score, when the children return to their teams, the child who finishes first and gets back to his team first gets two points, the child who finishes second gets one point. (If more teams are used, the child who gets back to his team first scores the number of points equal to the number of teams, for example if there are 4 teams, he earns 4 points. The second child to return to his team scores 3 points, the third child to return scores 2 points, and the last or fourth child scores 1 point.) The teacher gives another word, and the game continues in the same manner. Points are scored for each word given according to the order of the children from the different teams in completing the task.

Application:

Children are able to reinforce their auditory discrimination of initial sounds in words and associate them with initial position letters in printed words. Children need emphasis on the sound-symbol relationship of letters within the context of words.

Concept: Recognition of Visual Letter Patterns—Vowel Sound Principles (Open, Closed, Final *e*)

Activity: Letter Pattern Change

The children remain in their seats. Each child is given a card with a single-syllable word having one of the three vowel sound patterns (Examples: open-syllable pattern—*a, he, go;* closed-syllable pattern—*get, bud, hip;* final *e* pattern—*game, lute, side).* The teacher then holds up a word card with words also representing these patterns. Those children having words with the same letter pattern and the same vowel run to the board and write their word on the board and say it. Each child who is correct scores a point. Children may keep their own scores. Word cards should be changed frequently among the children. Later, the teacher may have the children come to the board whose word has the same letter pattern without it having to have the same vowel.

Application:

This game provides children the opportunity to practice recognition of visual letter patterns as cues to vowel sounds. Children can be called upon to identify the name of the vowel sound principle that their word represents, for example open, closed, or final *e*. The vowel digraph letter pattern might also be included in this activity.

Concept: Plurals of Nouns

Activity: Plural Relay

The class is divided into teams which stand in rows ten to fifteen feet from the blackboard. Each team has a different list of nouns placed on the board. On a signal the first child runs to the board and writes the plural of the first noun next to it. He returns to the rear of his team, and the second child runs to the board and writes the plural of the second noun, and so on. The child who is having difficulty may call upon one of the members of his team to help him. The team who finishes first with all the plurals written correctly wins. At first, lists of nouns may just include regular plurals; later, words with irregular noun plurals may be added.

Application:

This activity enables children to practice their skills in identifying plural forms of nouns. As irregular noun plurals are worked with, the children can be helped to note that not all nouns have the same plural endings. They can be helped to note that some nouns form their plurals by changing their spelling and that some nouns remain the same for the plural form.

Concept: Inflectional Endings—*s, ed, ing*
Activity: Ending Relay

The class is divided into teams. Each team is given a box filled with sight vocabulary words having *s, ed,* and *ing* endings. The boxes are placed by a blackboard. The teams make rows at a staring line ten to fifteen feet from the blackboard. On a signal the first child of each team runs to the team's box and picks out three words, one with an *s* ending, one with *ed,* and one with *ing* ending. He places the words along the chalk tray, pronounces each, and returns to his team. The second child continues in the same manner. If a child is having difficulty, he may call upon one member of his team to help him. The team that finishes with the accurate selection and pronunciation of words first wins.

Application:

This game enables children to practice their skills in identifying visually presented words with different inflectional endings. The game may later include words with irregular endings. This activity also provides reinforcement of sight vocabulary.

Concept: Dividing Words Into Syllables
Activity: Syllable Relay

The children are divided into two teams. A captain is chosen for each team. The teams stand about fifteen feet from a finish line. Each team is given a set of cards that have individual letters written on them. Each captain is given a red card. The teacher holds up a card with a two-syllable word written on it large enough for all to see. If the two-syllable word contains five letters, the first five children on each team look for the correct letters in their set of cards, run to the finish line, and stand, holding their letters in correct order to spell the word. The captain then stands with his red card between the letters where the word is divided into syllables. The team making up the word with the proper designation for dividing it into syllables first scores a point The next word is then given. The next children on the team find the necessary letters and proceed in the same manner. The team with the highest score wins.

Application:

When children have had work with the syllabication rules (vc/cv, v/cv, and v/c*le*), this game can provide the necessary drill for reinforcing these rules. Those children having difficulty can be helped to see the vowel-consonant patterns in the words as they group themselves as letters and how the words are divided into syllables. In this game the children having difficulty are helped by other members of the team rather than being eliminated.

Concept: Accent as Cues to Meaning
Activity: Accent Relay

The class is divided into several teams. The teams make rows behind a starting line ten to fifteen feet from a blackboard. Complete sets of words (a few more than the number of children on the teams), divided into syllables and marked with accents, are written on the board. Examples of words to be used are *ob'ject* and *object'*, *re'cord* and *record'*, *per'mit* and *permit'*. The teacher reads a sentence in which one of the words from the board is used. The first child on each team runs to the board and underlines the correct word as it was used in the teacher's sentence. He then returns to the rear of his team. The first child to return to his team scores a point for his team. The second child proceeds to underline a second word with the teacher's reading of another sentence. This procedure continues until each child has an opportunity to participate. The team with the most points wins. At any time a child is having difficulty, he may ask one member of his team for help.

Application:

This game helps children to listen carefully to words in the context of a sentence for clues to meaning. Children can also be helped to note the change of the function of these words in sentences when there is an accent change, that of moving from a noun to a verb function.

Concept: Alphabetical Order
Activity: Alphabet Relay

The children are divided into several teams. Word lists are written on the board for each team with as many words as there are team members. There should be different words in each list. The teams make rows behind a starting line ten to fifteen feet from the blackboard. On a signal the first child on each team runs to the board and writes the number 1 in front of the first word in alphabetical order. Upon returning to the rear of his team, the second child runs and puts number 2 in front of the second word to come in alphabetical order. This procedure is continued until all the words are numbered in proper alphabetical order. The first team completing its list correctly wins. The difficulty of the alphabetizing task can be increased by using words with the same first letter, then the same first two letters, and so on. A child who is having difficulty may seek the help from one member of his team.

Application:

This highly motivating activity provides children with the necessary repetition for developing skills of alphabetizing words. The nature of the competition also puts emphasis on quickness in using this skill as an aid to finding words in a dictionary in a minimum amount of time.

Concept: Alphabetical Order
Activity: Alphabet Line-Up

The class is divided into two teams. For each team a set of twenty-six cards, one with each letter of the alphabet, is placed out of order on the chalk tray at the front of the room or pinned to a bulletin board. The teams make rows at a specified distance from the letter display. A goal line is established at the back of the room for each team. The object of the game is for each member, one at a time, to run to pick a letter in correct alphabetical order, carry it to the team's goal line, and place the letters side by side in correct order. When each team member has found a letter, the team begins again until the alphabet is complete. The first team to complete placing the alphabet correctly at its goal line wins.

Application:

Children need many different types of opportunity to practice putting the letters in correct alphabetical order. This game provides a new activity to practice this skill.

Concept: Alphabetical Order
Activity: Jumping Rope

The children are divided into several teams, each with a jump rope. As two children from each team turn the rope, each child is given a chance to jump rope to the rhythm of the following verse:

> Ice cream soda,
> Delaware punch,
> Tell me the name
> Of your honey bunch.
> Her name begins with A-B-C- . . .

When the jumper misses, he tries to think of a girl's name (a girl tries to think of a boy's name) beginning with the letter on which he missed. If the child can think of a name, he scores one point for his team. The child then becomes a rope turner. Each child should be given a chance at jumping. The team with the highest score within a specified amount of time wins.

Application:

The children can be encouraged to say the alphabet along with the jumper. This type of activity enables every child to get the necessary repetition to identify letters in alphabetical order. Those having difficulty are helped by the rest of the group without attention being called to them.

Concept: Alphabetical Order
Activity: Alphabet Throw

The children are divided into teams. A series of five circles twelve inches in diameter are drawn in front of each group. One letter of the alphabet is marked in each circle. The letters in the circles need not necessarily be placed in correct order, but they should be a series of letters (A,B,C,D,E or H,I,J,K,L). Each group is given five beanbags numbered from one to five. Each team stands in a row behind a line about six to ten feet from the circles. On a signal the first child of each team throws his number one beanbag toward the circle with the first letter according to its alphabetical order, then the second, and so on. One point is given for each bag that lands within the circle in correct alphabetical order (bag 1 in A, bag 2 in B, bag 3 in C, and so on). The child then takes up the bags and runs to the rear of the line, giving the bags to the next child on the team as he passes. When all the children have had the chance to throw, the team having the highest score wins.

Application:

In this game the children are provided the practice in using their skills in putting letters in alphabetical order. By changing the letters after each game, the children become familiar with various parts of the alphabet. When changing letters, the teacher might add and delete only a couple of letters rather than using a complete new set of letters.

Concept: Guide Words in Dictionary

Activity: Where Is The Word

The class is divided into teams. Cards are made up with different sets of guide words printed on them large enough for all children to see. The words *Before, On,* and *After* are written on the board in front of each team. The teams make rows ten to fifteen feet from the blackboard. The teacher selects one of the sets of guide words and displays it where everyone can see it. The teacher then holds up a word printed on a card. The first child on each team then runs to the board and puts a check mark under one of the three words, depending on whether the word the teacher is holding would come *before, on,* or *after* the page with the guide words being used. The first child to check the correct answer on the board scores a point for his team. A child may seek the help of one member of his team for his word the teacher has displayed. After scoring a point for a team, the teacher then displays another word, and the second child continues in the same manner. The team with the highest score wins. A new set of guide words is then used.

Application:

Children are able to practice their skills in using guide words in an exciting situation. At first the teacher can use words with different first letters to make the task easier. Later, words can require use of the first two, three, and four letters to determine whether the word would appear on that page. The teacher can group children with some teams competing against each other using the less complex tasks and other teams competing by working with the more complex skills.

Sight Vocabulary

Concept: Sight Vocabulary

Activity: Word Carpet (Variation)

Several squares are drawn on the floor or pieces of paper are placed on the floor to represent Magic Carpets. Each Magic Carpet is numbered one to three to correspond with a numbered list of words on the blackboard. The words include new vocabulary from the children's experience stories, readers, and social studies or science units. Two teams of children are selected, and each team forms a chain by holding hands. To music, the two teams march around in circles and back and forth in a zig-zag manner over the Magic Carpet until the music stops. Each child then standing on or closest to a Magic Carpet identifies any word from the numbered list on the board that corresponds with the number at that Magic Carpet. The teacher then erases that word from the list, if it is read correctly. Each team scores one point for any correctly identified word. The team with the highest score wins.

Application:

This game provides an interesting activity whereby new words are given additional emphasis. To focus on meaning of new words, the teacher can require the child who has read a word correctly to put it in a sentence in order for the team to score an additional point. Children can also be helped to identify specific word analysis clues they used to identify their words.

Concept: Sight Vocabulary
Activity: Call Phrase

The children form a circle, facing the center. They may be seated or standing. One child is designated as the Caller and stands in the center of the circle. Each child is given a card with a phrase printed on it. Several children can have the same phrase. The Caller draws a card from a box containing corresponding phrase cards and holds up the card for everyone to see. When he reads the phrase, this is the signal for those children in the circle with the same phrase to exchange places before the Caller can fill in one of the vacant places in the circle. The remaining child becomes the Caller.

Application:

Children need opportunities to develop quick recognition of phrases. This game provides the repetition necessary to help children develop familiarity with phrases they are meeting in their reading material. The phrases may be taken from group experience stories, readers, or children's own experience stories.

Concept: Sight Vocabulary

Activity: Word Steps

A goal line is drawn on the surface area at the opposite end of the play area from where half the class is standing. The rest of the children are observers. The teacher holds up a word card and calls a child's name. If the child can identify the word, he moves forward by taking the number of hops (taking off and landing on same foot) indicated by the number on the back of the word card. Words selected for the word cards come from experience stories and basic readers. If the child does not know the word, any child who is observing may raise his hand to call the word. If he is correct, he takes that child's place and moves forward. Any child who is eliminated in this manner can later volunteer a word to get back in the game. The first child to reach the goal line is the winner.

Application: (Follows this section of activities for reinforcement of sight vocabulary inasmuch as the application is the same.)

Concept: Sight Vocabulary
Activity: Word Toss

Three columns of words from stories in basal readers, experience stories, and Dolch Word Lists or other word lists are written on the board. Each column is numbered 1, 2, and 3, according to the points to be earned by identifying a word in that column. Each column contains as many words as there are children in the game. Three circles are then drawn on the surface area and marked 1, 2, and 3. The class is divided into a number of teams. Each team stands in a row about ten feet from the circles and is given a beanbag. On a signal the first child on each team tosses his beanbag at one of the circles. If he misses, he gets one extra toss. Whatever numbered circle the beanbag lands on, the child may select any word to read from the word column with that number. If he reads it correctly, he earns one, two, or three points for his team, according to the number of the column from which he read the word. That word is then erased from the column. The game continues until each child has an opportunity to toss for a word. The team with the highest score wins.

Application: (Follows this section of activities for reinforcement of sight vocabulary.)

Concept: Sight Vocabulary
Activity: Word Erase

The children are divided into several teams. The teams make rows at a specified distance from a blackboard. Previously, the teacher has written lists of words from children's experience stories and readers, one for each team. On a signal the first child on each team calls the first word. If he is correct, as determined by the teacher, he runs to the board and erases it, then returns to the rear of his team. If he does not know the word, he may ask for help from one member of his team. The second child continues in the same manner. The game is won by the first team finished.

Application. (Follows this section of activities for reinforcement of sight vocabulary.)

Concept: Sight Vocabulary
Activity: Words In A Circle

The children stand in a circle, facing in. Each child is given a word card with a word from experience stories, basals, or word lists. Each child places his card on the surface area. If outdoors and the day is windy, place a stone on the card. At the teacher's direction the children may skip, hop, or march around the cards in the circle until a signal is given to stop. Then, each child in turn reads the word he is standing by. When each child has read his own word, the group moves again about the circle until the next signal to stop. Each time a child can read the word he is standing by, he scores a point. If a child cannot read his word, the children on either side may help him. The first child to score five points is the winner. Later, the teacher may use sentence cards for the children to read.

Application: (Follows this section of activities for reinforcement of sight vocabulary.)

Concept: Sight Vocabulary
Activity: Squirrel With A Nut

All the children except one sit at their desks with heads resting on an arm as though sleeping but with one hand outstretched. The extra child is the Squirrel. The Squirrel, who carries a nut (words on cards shaped like a nut), runs quietly about the room and drops a nut into the open hand of a child. The child jumps up from his seat, pronounces the word, and chases the Squirrel, who is safe only when he reaches his nest (his seat). If the Squirrel gets in his nest without being caught, he may be the Squirrel again. Otherwise, the child who catches him becomes the Squirrel, or the teacher may select another child to be the Squirrel.

Application:

Words selected for these games may come from experience stories and stories read on that or the previous day. These games provide the necessary repetition to develop instant recognition of words and can be used to maintain words in addition to word banks and word games that the children utilize in the classroom.

Comprehension

Concept: Following Directions
Activity: Simon Says

The children stand about the play area facing the person who plays Simon. Every time Simon says to do something, the children must do it. However, if a command is given without the prefix "Simon says," the children must remain motionless. For example, when "Simon says take two steps," everyone must take two steps. But if Simon says, "Walk backwards two steps," no one should move. If a child moves at the wrong time or turns in the wrong direction, the child puts one hand on his head. The second time he misses, he puts the other hand on his head. The third time he fails, he is out. The more quickly the commands are given and the greater number of commands, the more difficult the game will be. The last child remaining is the winner.

Application:

This activity provides children the opportunity to follow oral directions in a highly motivating situation. The rules of the game, as adapted, allow those children who need the practice additional chances to remain in the game for a longer period of time. It might be desirable to divide the class into teams, with the team having the largest number still in the game after a specified period of time, the winner.

Concept: Following Directions

Activity: Do This, Do That

Flash cards of "Do This" and "Do That" are used in this game. One child is selected to be the leader and stands in front of the group. The teacher holds up a flash card, and the leader makes a movement such as walking in place, running in place, swinging his arms, or hopping. The children follow the actions of the leader when the sign says "Do This." When the teacher holds up the sign "Do That," the children must not move although the leader continues the action. A point is scored against the child who is caught moving. The object of the game is to get the lowest score possible. The leader can be exchanged frequently.

Application:

This game can be used to help children to read carefully in order to follow directions. Later, this game can be adapted by having the leader display written directions on flash cards, for example hop in place, jump once, walk in place, and the like.

Concept: Classification
Activity: Pet Store

One fairly large Pet Store is marked off at one end of the playing area and a Home at the other end. At the side is a Cage. In the center of the playing area stands the Pet Store Owner. All the children stand in the Pet Store and are given a picture of one kind of pet (for example, fish, bird, dog). There should be about two or three pictures of each kind of pet. The Pet Store Owner calls "Fish" (or any of the other pets in the game). The children who have pictures of fish must try to run from the Pet Store to their new Home without being caught or tagged by the Owner. If they are caught, they must go to the cage and wait for the next game. The game continues until all the Pets have tried to get to their new home. Kinds of pets can be changed frequently.

Application:

By grouping themselves according to the animal pictures, children are able to practice classifying things that swim, things that fly, and so forth. At the end of the game the class can count how many fish, dogs, and so forth were caught. All the fish, birds, dogs, and so forth can then form their own line to *swim, fly,* or *walk* back to the Pet Store, where new pictures can be given to the children for another game.

Concept: Classification
Activity: Ducks Fly

Children stand at their seats. One of them may be the leader. At the first-grade level it might, in some cases, be better for the teacher to be the leader. The leader faces the class. He names different things that can fly, as ducks, birds, airplanes. As the leader calls out "Ducks fly, Birds fly, Airplanes fly," he moves his arms as if flying. The class follows as long as he names something that can fly. If he says, "Elephants fly," and although the leader continues to keep his arms moving as if flying, the children must stop moving their arms. Those who are caught flying have a point scored against them. If the arms get tired, the leader might try things that walk, swim, and so forth, and the children then make the appropriate movement. The child with the lowest score wins.

Application:

Children need to develop the skill of classifying things into groups having common characteristics. Children should be helped to note that some animals actually can do several of the movements named as flying, walking, and/or swimming. Later, children can collect pictures of animals and make a display of animals who walk, swim, and the like.

Concept: Vocabulary Meaning
Activity: Match The Meaning

The children are divided into several teams. The teams make rows ten to fifteen feet from the blackboard. Meanings of words are written on the board ahead of time, a group of definitions for each team. Each child is given a card with a word that matches a meaning on the board. A few extra definitions are included in each list on the board. On a signal the first child runs to the board and erases the meaning that defines his word. The child may seek the help of his team before going to the board. The teacher checks each child before he erases a definition. It the child still has selected a definition that is incorrect, he must return to his team so they can decide what is the correct definition. Each child proceeds in the same manner until every child has identified the definition of his word and has returned to his team. The first team finished wins.

Application:

Emphasis needs to be placed on word meanings when developing sight vocabulary. This game provides an exciting and highly motivating means of providing drill with meanings, and children are able to help each other in developing word meanings. This activity may be set up for specific reading groups to reinforce words they are meeting in their stories.

Concept: Vocabulary Meaning
Activity: Word Hunt

The children are divided into several teams. The teacher has a box of pictures and a set of word cards corresponding to the pictures for each team. The word sets are placed in a flat box by a sentence chart set up for each team. Each child on a team selects a picture from the team's box. The teams make rows ten to fifteen feet from their sentence charts. On a signal the first child of each team goes to the word-set box, looks for the word to match his picture, and then places the picture and the word on the sentence chart. He then returns to his team and taps the next child. The second child proceeds in the same manner until everyone has matched a picture and word. The team finishing first gets one point plus one point for each correctly matched word and picture.

Application:

Emphasis on word meaning is provided in this game. Children need opportunities in many settings to build a meaningful sight vocabulary. Children in this activity are helped to visualize the concept that a word represents through pictures.

Concept: Vocabulary Meaning—Colors
Activity: Rainbow

The children form a circle, facing the center. The children may be seated or standing. One child is designated the Caller and stands in the center of the circle. Instead of counting off by numbers, the children are given a small piece of paper of one of the basic colors. The Caller is given a set of word cards, one for each of the basic colors corresponding to the colors given the children in the circle. The Caller selects one word card and shows it. The children with this color attempt to change places while the Caller tries to get to one of the vacant places in the circle. The remaining child becomes the new Caller. The Caller may show two word cards. Those children with the two colors then run to change places with the Caller again, trying to get to one of the vacant places in the circle. At any time the Caller or teacher may call out "rainbow." When this call is given, everyone must change to a different position.

Application:

Children need many opportunities to develop their recognition of words in games of this nature in which they are associating the word with the concept the word represents. This game can be simplified in order for it to become appropriate for a language development activity. The Caller can have just color cards matching those of the children. Later, when the children have learned to match colors, the Caller can call out the names of the colors.

Concept: Vocabulary Meaning—Action Words and Days of the week

Activity: The Mulberry Bush

The children form a circle, facing in. The teacher may write the days of the week on the board in proper order and go over them with the children before the rhythmic activity is begun. The teacher can also talk with the children about how they would do the various tasks involved in the various verses. As the verses are sung, the children act out the action of the words.

> Here we go round the mulberry bush,
> The mulberry bush, the mulberry bush,
> Here we go round the mulberry bush,
> So early in the morning.
> This is the way we wash our clothes,
> Wash our clothes, wash our clothes,
> This is the way we wash our clothes,
> So early Monday morning.
> This is the way we iron our clothes,
> etc.
> So early Tuesday morning.
> This is the way we mend our clothes,
> etc.
> So early Wednesday morning.
> This is the way we scrub the floor,
> etc.
> So early Thursday morning.
> This is the way we sweep the house,
> etc.
> So early Friday morning.
> This is the way we bake our bread,
> etc.
> So early Saturday morning.
> This is the way we go to church,
> etc.
> So early Sunday morning.

Application:

This rhythmic activity helps children to recall the days of the week in their proper order. It also helps children to develop the concept that words represent action or behavior of people that can be observed, as well as names of specific objects.

Concept Vocabulary Meaning—Left and Right

Activity: Changing Seats

Enough chairs for each child in the group are placed side by side in about four or five rows. The children sit alert, ready to move either way. The teacher calls, "Change right!" and each child moves into a seat to his right. When the teacher calls "Change left!" each child moves left. The child at the end of the row who does not have a seat to move to must run to the other end of his row to sit in the vacant seat there. The teacher can bring excitement to the game by the quickness of commands or unexpectedness by calling the same direction several times in succession. After each command the first row of children who all find seats may score a point for that row.

Application:

This type of activity makes children more aware of the necessity of differentiating left from right. At the beginning of the game, children may not be able to differentiate directions rapidly. The teacher will need to gear the rapidity of her commands according to the skills of the group.

Concept: Vocabulary Meaning—Over and Under

Activity: Over And Under Relay

The children are divided into several teams. The children stand one behind the other, separated about one foot apart. A ball is given to the captain of each team, who stands at the head of the row. On a signal the captain passes the ball behind him over his head and calls "over." The second in line takes the ball and passes it between his legs and calls "under." Number three in line takes and passes the ball over his head and calls "over" and so on down the line until the last one in line receives the ball. He then runs to the head of the line and starts passing the ball back in the same manner. The team whose captain reaches the head of the file first wins.

Application:

This game helps children to dramatize the meaning of the words *over* and *under*. For a variation the teacher can hold up a card with either *over* or *under* written on it to indicate how the first child on each team should start passing the ball or how the ball should be passed by the child moving forward to the front of the team.

Concept: Vocabulary Meaning—North, South, East, West
Activity: Weather Bureau

The children may stand by their desks. One child is selected as Weatherman and calls the direction of the winds. For example, if the Weatherman calls "The wind blows South," all the children turn quickly to the south. They turn in the direction of east if he calls "The wind blows East." Whenever the Weatherman calls out "Tornado," the children turn three times in place and sit. The last child to sit has two points scored against him. Any child turning in the wrong direction gets one point against him. The children keep their own scores. The child with the lowest score wins. The children may take turns being Weatherman.

Application:

By dramatizing the directions, children are helped to develop understanding of the concept of compass directions. The teacher may facilitate directions for the children by helping them to correctly place the letters *N, S, E, W* about the room to give compass directions appropriate for a given classroom with the aid of a compass.

Concept: Vocabulary Meaning—Action Words
Activity: Word Action

The children sit in a group. A number of action words are printed on cards and placed in a box. These words have been previously introduced through the children's experience stories and readers. One child will take a card from the box, read it silently to himself, and show it to the teacher. He then proceeds to dramatize the word. If the child does not know the word, the teacher tells him. The children are reminded not to read the word with their lips, which might give it away to the others. As the child acts out the word, the other children raise their hands and try to guess the word. When a child guesses the correct word, he acts out the next word.

Application:

This activity helps children to gain the meaning of words by providing them means of visualizing and feeling the action represented by a word. Each child can gain the concept that words represent not only specific objects they can see and touch but also actions that can be observed.

Concept: Vocabulary Meaning—Action Words
Activity: What To Play

The children may stand beside their desks. One of the children is selected to be the leader. While that child is coming to the front of the room to lead, the rest of the class begins to sing:

> Mary tell us what to play,
> What to play, what to play.
> Mary tell us what to play,
> Tell us what to play.

(The song is sung to the tune of Mary Had a Little Lamb.) The leader then says, "Let's play we're fishes," or "Let's wash dishes," or "Let's hold a doll." She then performs some action that the other children have to imitate. On a signal the children stop, and a new leader is selected.

Application:

This game gives children an opportunity to act out the meanings of words. It helps them to recognize that spoken words represent actions of people as well as things that can be touched.

Concept: Vocabulary Meaning—Action Words
Activity: Action Relay

The children divide into several teams. The teams make rows ten to fifteen feet from a blackboard. The teacher makes duplicate lists for each team with as many action words on the board for each team as there are team members. The first child on each team, on a signal, runs to the board, crosses out the first word, calls it out, and does what the word says as he returns to his team and touches the next child. The second child proceeds in the same manner until every child has demonstrated a word. Any child who cannot figure out his word can ask one member of his team to help him. The first team to complete the acting out of each word correctly, wins.

Application:

This game helps children to build meanings or words by having them dramatize the words. This helps children to visualize the meanings of words. Children who are having difficulty should not be eliminated from the game but should receive help from the other children.

Concept: Vocabulary Meaning—Word Opposites

Activity: Word Change

The class is divided into two teams who line up at opposite ends of the playing area. Each child is given a word printed on a card. The words given to one team are the word opposites of the words given to the other team. One child is selected to be *it* and stands in the middle of the play area. The teacher calls out a word, and this word and its opposite run and try to exchange places. *It* attempts to get into one of the vacated places before the two children can exchange places. The remaining child becomes *it* for the next time.

Application:

This activity focuses on the meaning of sight vocabulary words. This game can be varied with emphasis on synonyms, with teams given words that are similar in meaning.

Concept: Vocabulary Meaning—Word Opposites

Activity: I'm Tall, I'm Small

The children form a circle with one child in the center. The child in the center of the circle stands with his eyes closed. It may be helpful to have the child blindfolded. The children in the circle walk slowly around the circle singing or saying the following verse:

> I'm tall, I'm very small,
> I'm small, I'm very tall,
> Sometimes I'm tall,
> Sometimes I'm small,
> Guess what I am now.

As the children walk and sing "tall," "very tall," or "small," or "very small," they stretch up or stoop down, depending on the words. At the end of the singing the teacher signals the children in the circle to assume a stretching or stooping position. The child in the center, still with eyes closed, guesses which position they have taken. For the next game another child is selected to be in the center.

Application:

This activity helps children to develop word meaning by acting out the words. Use of word opposites in this manner helps to dramatize the differences in the meaning of words. The words and actions can be changed to incorporate a larger number of "opposites," for example:

> My hands are near, my hands are far,
> Now they're far, now they're near,
> Sometimes they're near,
> Sometimes they're far,
> Guess what they are now.

Concept:　Vocabulary Meaning—Word Opposites

Activity:　Opposite Relay

The children are divided into several teams. The teams stand in rows behind a line ten to fifteen feet from a blackboard. The teacher displays a word on a card printed large enough for all to see it. The first child on each team runs to the board and writes the first letter of the word opposite and returns to the rear of his team. The second team member then runs to the board and adds the second letter of the word opposite. This continues until the word opposite has been completed. The first team to complete the correct word opposite spelled accurately scores a point. The team members can discuss among themselves what the word opposite will be and how to spell the word. The teacher displays another word, and the next child on the team begins the writing of the first letter of the word opposite. The game proceeds then in the same manner. The team with the most points wins. In cases where teams use different but correct word opposites, the first team to complete their word accurately spelled scores a point.

Application:

In this activity children have the opportunity to work with meaning of words. Because there is team decision-making in determining the word opposite and its spelling, the slower children are able to remain in the game and are aided in their learning by the more-able learner.

Concept: Sequence of Events
Activity: Sentence Relay

Relay teams of five children each are selected to make rows before a starting line ten to fifteen feet from sentence charts for each team. The remaining children can serve as scorers. Each child on the teams is given a sentence that fits into an overall sequence for the five sentences given a team. (The teams are given duplicate sentences.) Each sentence gives a clue to its position in the sentence sequence, either by idea content or word clue. On a given signal the team members get together and decide the correct sentence order. The child with the first sentence then runs to the sentence chart, places his sentence on the top line of the chart, and returns to his team. The child with the next sentence then runs to place his sentence below the first sentence. This procedure continues until the sentences are in order. The team to complete the story with sentences in correct order first wins. The scorers check on the accuracy of the sentence order for each team. For the next game the scorers can exchange places with those who were on teams. Variations of this game can include the use of cartoons with each child on a team being given one frame of the cartoon strip. To make the game more difficult, more sentences may be added to the sequence. To prevent copying, the teacher can give different story sentences to each team.

Application:

In this game those children having difficulty with reading are helped by those who are more able readers and not eliminated from the game. After each game the teacher should go over key elements in the sentences that provided clues to the proper sequence.

Chapter Six

Teaching Slow Learners Mathematics Through Active Games

The use of games in number experiences of children has long been recognized. In one section of his "Laws," the suggestion is made by Plato that "Teachers mix together objects adapting the rules of elementary arithmetic in play." The opportunities for such procedures as counting, computing, and measuring abound in many of the active game experiences of the child in present-day society. In certain types of games such as tag games, children caught can be counted and compared to the number not caught. In those kinds of games requiring scoring, there are opportunities for counting, adding, and subtracting. In fact, it would be difficult to identify any kind of active game situation where some sort of quantitative factors are not involved.

In using the active game approach, teachers should become aware of all the mathematics experiences children might have in these activities. Besides experiences in counting and comparing scores, there are opportunities in keeping records which can be used to develop concepts of averages, percentages, charts, and graphs. These games provide natural situations to practice the skills involved in a meaningful way. For upper elementary children, team or group standings on a won and lost basis can be utilized to work with decimals and percentages. Team or individual standings can be determined by dividing the number of games won (or hits made) by the number of games played (or hits attempted). Thus, if a child made three successful throws out of four attempts, four is divided into three, giving a percentage of .750. Graphs and charts can be developed by the children to show team or individual progress. A graph or chart can be made over a period of several days or weeks indicating how well a team or child performed in a particular task and improvement made.

Establishing boundaries and dimensions for games helps to develop and reinforce measurement, scale, and area concepts. Children can work from scale plans of boundaries for different games in order to mark off the necessary dimensions for the games to be played.

Organizing a group to play a game provides meaningful problems to be solved using mathematics concepts and skills. The teacher can pose such questions as, "If we divide the class into three teams, what part of the class would each team be?" or "If we need ten children for a team, how can we divide?"

As previously mentioned, after a game has been played, it should be evaluated not only in terms of children's reaction to the game and how it was played but also in terms of how well the children understand the mathematics concepts inherent in the game or have developed the skills involved.

The following games in the chapter have been grouped by major areas of the elementary school mathematics curriculum. The summation of each game elaborates on the inherent mathematics concept or number skills involved. Some of the games are particularly useful for introducing and developing a mathematics concept. These games involve the learner actively and provide the child the opportunity to dramatize the concept physically. Other games reinforce a concept and develop skills by providing the repetitive drill children need but in an interesting and personally involving situation.

The application section for each game indicates the nature of that activity. The teacher is provided suggestions for using the game to develop the concept inherent in that activity. If the game is more appropriate for reinforcement of a concept previously developed, the application section specifies the skills being developed through practice and use in a highly motivating situation. The teacher will want to adapt many of the games to develop mathematics concepts or practice arithmetic skills other than the ones utilized in the games.

CLASSIFICATION OF GAMES ACCORDING TO MAJOR AREAS IN ELEMENTARY SCHOOL MATHEMATICS

The following is a summary of the active games that contain mathematics concepts and skills. Descriptions of the games follow the summary.

Concept	*Game*
Number System:	
Quantitative Aspects of Numbers and Numeral Recognition	Hot Spot I Want To Meet Watch The Numbers
Quantitative Aspects of Numbers and Counting	Bee Sting Count The Pins Count And Go Muffin Man Fish Net Ten Little Indians Round Up Chain Tag Card Toss Ball Bounce Mrs. Brown's Mouse Trap Come With Me Ball Pass Cowboys And Indians (Space Men And Moon Men) Number Man
Counting	Count, Move, And Stop Pick-Up Race Pass Ball Relay Bouncing Relay Red Light
Number Line	Number Line Relay
Ordinal Numbers	Leader Ball Fetch And Carry (Rescue Relay) The Number Race Call And Catch

Concept	Game
Numeral Recognition Beyond One Hundred	Postman Game
Roman Numerals	Roman Numeral Relay
	Roman Numeral Bounce

Addition:

Three Deep
Back To Back
Addition Tag
Beanbag Throw (Variation)
Add-A-Number Relay
Beanbag Toss
Number Catch
Steal The Bacon (Variation)
Space Demon
Number Man (Variation)
Arithmetic Relay

Word Symbols in a Number Sentence	Lions And The Hunters
Place Value of 1's, 10's, 100's	Bundle Relay
Place Value With Zero as a Place Holder	Place Value Relay

Subtraction:

Ten Little Birds
Take Away, Take Away
Musical Chairs
Ten Little Chickadees
Dodge Ball
Animal Catch
Cheese And Mice
Tossing Darts

(See Section on Addition)	Number Catch
(See Section on Addition)	Steal The Bacon (Variation)
(See Section on Addition)	Space Demon

Concept	Game
(See Section on Addition)	Number Man (Variation)
(See Section on Addition)	Arithmetic Relay

Multiplication:

	Call Ball (Variation)
	Twice As Many
	Grand March
(See Section on Addition)	Number Catch
(See Section on Addition)	Steal The Bacon (Variation)
(See Section on Addition)	Space Demon
(See Section on Addition)	Number Man (Variation)
(See Section on Addition)	Arithmetic Relay

Division:

	Triplet Tag
	Birds Fly South
	Birds Fly South (Variation)
	Beanbag Throw
(See Section on Addition)	Number Catch
(See Section on Addition)	Steal The Bacon (Variation)
(See Section on Addition)	Space Demon
(See Section on Addition)	Number Man (Variation)
(See Section on Addition)	Arithmetic Relay

Fractions:

	Corner Spry
	Hit Or Miss
	Flannelboard Fractions
	End Ball
	Fraction Target Relay
	Hit The Target
	Train Dodge
	Fraction Race

Decimals:

	Roving Decimal Point
	Dash Relay

Concept	*Game*
Measurement:	
Linear Measurement	Ring Toss
	Add-A-Jump Relay
Liquid Measurement	Milkman Tag
Telling Time	Tick Tock
	Set The Clock Relay
	Five Minute Relay
	Clock Race
Geometry:	
	Straight-Crooked Relay
	Around The Horn
	Run Circle Run
	Three Bounce Relay
	Streets And Alleys
	Jump The Shot
	Triangle Run
	Geometric Figure Relay
Monetary System:	
	Stepping Stones
	Name The Coin
	Bank
	Banker And The Coins

Number System

Concept: Quantitative Aspects of Numbers and Numeral Recognition

Activity: Hot Spot

Pieces of paper with numerals from one to ten are placed in various spots around the floor or play area. There should be several pieces of paper with the same numerals. The teacher has a number of large posters with various numbers of different objects on them. (The overhead projector may be used to present the different quantities of objects.) A poster is shown to the class. The children must identify the number of objects on the poster and then run to that numeral on the floor. Any child who is left without a spot gets a point against him. Any child who has less than five points at the end of the period is considered a winner.

Application:

Children are helped to count objects and then to identify the numeral that represents that number. After the game the posters can be put on display around the room with the correct numerals by each one.

Concept: Quantitative Aspects of Numbers and Numeral Recognition

Activity: I Want To Meet

Ten cards are prepared so that each of the numerals one through ten will appear on one card only. Distribute these cards, one to a child. Then give to each of the other children a number of objects (such as pegs, cards, acorns, paper clips), making sure that each of the quantities one through ten is represented at least once. The teacher calls out a number, as four, and asks the child who holds the card having that numeral on it to go to the front of the room and hold his card for all to see. The child then says, "I want to meet all fours." The children with four objects hold them up. Someone counts them, and those who hold the correct number of objects join the child who is holding the card with the numeral 4 on it. They then run to a goal at the opposite end of the room. The first child to reach the goal scores a point. The game goes on with other numbers called for. From time to time the teacher should change the objects and cards held by the children. The first child to score a specified number of points wins.

Application:

This activity provides a personally involving and interesting situation to relate numerals with the quantitative aspect of numbers. Children can be helped to count out the number of objects they have.

Concept: Quantitative Aspects of Numbers and Numeral Recognition

Actvity: Watch The Numbers

Write the numerals *1, 2, 3, 4, 5, 6* on large sheets of paper, one numeral per sheet. Write the numerals large enough so the children marching around the room can read them. The children start by marching around the room to music in single file. At any time the teacher will hold up one of the numerals. If the numeral is two, the children find partners and continue marching. If the numeral is three, the children march in three's. Whenever a child does not secure a partner or becomes a part of the grouping, he goes to the sideline. When the next numeral appears, he rejoins the scramble to get into a correct formation.

Application:

Children in this game are able to act out the quantitative aspects of numbers by forming appropriate size groups for the numerals called.

Concept: Quantitative Aspects of Numbers and Counting
Activity: Bee Sting

Three children are bees. They are in their hives marked in chalk on the play area. The rest of the children are in the center of the designated play area. The bees run out and try to catch (sting) the children. When a child is caught, he must go to the bee's hive. When all the children are caught, each bee counts those in his hive. Different children should have a chance to be bees.

Application:

In this activity the children are provided another opportunity to practice counting. They can be helped to see the numbers of children caught by the bees in terms of being greater than and less than those caught by other bees. Children should note the quantitative aspects of numbers by counting and that the numbers called represent objects, in this case children.

Concept: Quantitative Aspects of Numbers and Counting
Activity: Count The Pins

Plastic bowling pins or milk cartons are set up at one end of the playing area. These pins are arranged with four on the back row, three on the next row, two on the next, and one on the front row. When set up, they form a triangle. Each child has two turns to roll a plastic bowling ball. He stands behind a line to roll. The total number of pins knocked down in these two rolls is his score.

Each child may have several turns in a game, and his total score is tallied.

Application:

Children count their pins knocked down with each roll. Some children may be able to figure out their score without counting each pin. The teacher may add the total game score for each child, but they should be helped to count out their scores to obtain a total score.

Concept: Quantitative Aspects of Numbers and Counting
Activity: Count And Go

The children line up on the long side of a rectangular hard surface court. There are parallel lines which are unequal distances apart drawn in chalk on the court. The teacher stands across from the children with number cards. The teacher holds up any card at random (numbers on the cards are from 1 to the total number in the group). The children must count the lines as they run, skip, and so on toward the teacher. (This should vary with the abilities of the group.) When the children get to the line that corresponds to the numeral on the card, they should stop and stand still. The child who reaches the far side first is the winner. To keep the group small, the girls might take a turn and the boys watch to see if they count correctly. Then they can change places with the boys for the next game.

Application:

This activity reinforces counting as the children move forward the varying number of lines designated by the teacher. Another dimension to this activity would extend meaning to the concept of subtraction. Directions could be presented such as *plus two* and *minus three,* and the children would then proceed to carry out these directions in terms of moving forward or backward. The children should be helped to understand that the numeral *3* represents a group of three steps forward or backward.

Concept: Quantitative Aspects of Numbers and Counting
Activity: Muffin Man

The children stand in a circle with two children standing in the circle facing each other. While the first verse is sung, the children in the center stand still with hands on hips. When the second verse is sung, "Yes I know the Muffin Man" and so on, the two children clasp hands and skip around the inside of the circle, singing "Two of us know the Muffin Man" and so on. At the end of the verse these two children stand in front of two new partners and repeat the first and second verses. The second verse is now sung: "Four of us know the Muffin Man" and son on. This procedure is repeated to eight, sixteen, and so on, depending on the size of the group.

> Oh, do you know the Muffin Man,
> the Muffin Man, the Muffin Man?
> Oh, do you know the Muffin Man
> who lives in Drury Lane?
> Yes, I know the Muffin Man,
> the Muffin Man, the Muffin Man.
> Yes, I know the Muffin Man
> who lives in Drury Lane.

Application:

This rhythmic activity provides children the opportunity to dramatize the grouping process in concrete number situations. Children might be helped between singing the verses to count out the numbers involved for the following verse. Number sentences might also be written on the blackboard.

Concept: Quantitative Aspects of Numbers and Counting
Activity: Fish Net

The class is divided into two teams. Each team chooses a captain. One team is the Net; the other is the Fish. At the start the teams stand behind two goal lines at the opposite ends of the playground, facing each other. When the teacher gives a signal, both teams run forward toward the center. The Net tries to catch as many Fish as possible by making a circle around them by holding hands. The Fish try to get out of the opening before the Net closes. They cannot go through the Net by going under the arms of the children, but if the Net breaks because the children let go of each other's hands, the Fish can go through that opening until the hands are joined again. The Fish are safe if they get to the opposite goal line without being caught in the Net. When the

Net has made its circle, the captain counts the number of Fish inside, and the score is recorded. The next time the teams change places. When each side has had a chance to be the Net three times, the game is over. The team with the highest score for all three times wins.

Application:

Children have the opportunity to count the number of fish caught each time. Counting, in such activities, acquires meaning for the children because they can relate number names to specific objects.

Concept: Quantitative Aspects of Numbers and Counting
Activity: Ten Little Indians

The children form a circle, all facing in. Ten children are selected to be Indians, and each one is given a number from one to ten. As the song is sung, the child whose number is called skips to the center of the circle. When the Ten Little Indians are in the center, the song is reversed. Again, each child leaves the center and returns to the circle as his number is called. Other children might become Indians, and the song is repeated.

> One little, two little, three little Indians,
> Four little, five little, six little Indians,
> Seven little, eight little, nine little Indians,
> Ten little Indians boys.
> Ten little, nine little, eight little Indians,
> etc.
> One little Indian boy.

Application:

Position and sequence of numbers is important in basic arithmetic concepts. In this rhythmic activity, children are helped to see the quantitative aspects of ordinal numbers. The subtraction concept may also be introduced through this activity.

Concept: Quantitative Aspects of Numbers and Counting
Activity: Round Up[1]

All but ten children of the group take places in a scattered formation on the play area. The ten children join hands and are

---

[1]Humphrey, James H.: *Child Learning Through Elementary School Physical Education.* Dubuque, Iowa, Wm. C. Brown Co., 1966, p. 194.

the Round-Up Crew. The other children are the Steers. On a signal the Round-Up Crew, with hands joined, chases the Steers and attempts to surround one or more of them. To capture a Steer, the two end children of the Round-Up Crew join hands. As the Steers are captured, the children count the number aloud. They may have to stop and count each time another child is caught. When the tenth child is captured, they become the Round-Up Crew, and the game continues.

Application:

This game enables children to apply number names in sequence to definite objects, in this case, children. It provides practice in counting when the children check the number of Steers caught up to that point in the game until they reach number ten.

Concept: Quantitative Aspects of Numbers and Counting
Activity: Chain Tag

One child is chosen as leader. The leader chooses another child to assist him, and the two join hands. They chase the other children, trying to tag one. When a child has been tagged, he takes his place between the two, and the chain grows. The first two, the leader and his assistant, remain at the ends throughout the game and are the only ones who can tag. When the chain surrounds a child, he may not break through the line or go under the hands. When the chain breaks, it must be reunited before the tagging begins again. The leader counts out loud every time he gets another child in his chain. The game ends when the chain has five or ten children. A new leader is chosen, who in turn proceeds in the same manner.

Application:

The children have practice in counting as each child is tagged. This activity helps to show the cardinal concept of numbers.

Concept: Quantitative Aspects of Numbers and Counting
Activity: Card Toss

The class is divided into several teams. A set of ten cards are made for each team. Each team member tosses the ten cards singly into a propped-up hat, wastebasket, or wide-mouth can about ten feet away. Each successful toss scores one point for the team. Each child counts the number of cards he tosses successfully into the container and reports the score to his team's scorekeeper. The children may be helped by the teacher to add the total score. Later, the children will be able to add their own team's total score.

Application:

This game provides a highly motivating activity for practicing counting and reinforcing the understanding of the quantitative aspects of numbers. Children should be encouraged to check the counting of the other members of the team as well as their own in order to give all the children the maximum opportunity to develop the skill of counting.

Concept: Quantitative Aspects of Numbers and Counting
Activity: Ball Bounce

Tape ten large paper squares to the floor, arranging them about fifteen inches apart. Number these squares from one to ten and put them in mixed order. Have the children sit in a circle and let the children take turns bouncing the ball on a square the same number of times as the numeral marked on the square. Each time a child does the complete set correctly, he scores a point. The other children can help to keep track to see if each child bounces the ball the correct number of times for each square.

Application:

All the children are encouraged to count the bounces of the other children in addition to their own turn with the ball. A child may be helped to count as he bounces the ball according to the numeral he has identified. It should be brought out that the numeral 5 represents the quantity 5 as the number of times the ball is bounced.

Concept: Quantitative Aspects of Numbers and Counting
Activity: Mrs. Brown's Mouse Trap[2]

Some of the children stand in a circle, facing in. The children hold hands up high to represent a mouse trap. The other children are Mice. On a signal the Mice go in and out of the circle. One child is Mrs. Brown. When she calls out "Snap!" the children in

---

[2]Humphrey, James H.: Teaching Children Mathematics Through Games, Rhythms, and Stunts. LP No. 5000, Deal, N. J., Kimbo Records, 1968.

the circle drop hands (still joined). As the mouse trap closes, some of the Mice are caught in the circle (the trap). The teacher helps the children count how many Mice were caught and how many were not caught. The children should exchange places for the next game.

Application:

In this activity children are able to relate numbers to specific objects and to practice counting. The teacher can help the children to identify different size groups and whether these groups are larger or smaller than each other.

Concept: Quantitative Aspects of Numbers and Counting
Activity: Come With Me[3]

The children stand close together in a circle. One child is *it*. *It* goes around the outside of the circle. *It* taps a child and says, "Come with me." That child follow *it*. *It* continues in the same manner, tapping children who then follow *it* as he goes around the outside of the circle. At any time *it* may call, "Go home!" All the children following *it*, and *it* himself, run to find a vacant place in the circle. The remaining child becomes *it* for the next game. At the beginning the teacher has the children count how many there are at the start. *It* can count the children as he taps them. All the children also can be encouraged to count as *it* tags children. The number of children not tagged might also be counted.

Application:

The children are able to practice counting varying size groups in this activity. By having *it* and all the children count as the children are tagged, each child is helped to see number names related to specific objects.

Concept: Quantitative Aspects of Numbers and Counting
Activity: Ball Pass[4]

The children are divided into two teams, and both teams form one single circle. If the group is large, the teacher may have two circles with two teams in each circle. The teacher gives directions for a ball to be passed or tossed from one child to another. The

---

[3]*Ibid.*

[4]Humphrey, James H.: *Child Learning Through Elementary School Physical Education.* Dubuque, Iowa, Wm. C. Brown Co., 1966, p. 129.

teacher calls, "Pass the ball to the right, toss the ball to the left over two children," varying the calls by the numbers and direction given. The game may be complicated by using more than one ball of different sizes and weights. If a child drops a ball, a point is scored against his team. The team with the lowest score wins.

Application:

The tasks in this activity provide children practice in relating numbers to specific quantities which they act out and in identifying right and left.

Concept: Quantitative Aspects of Numbers and Counting
Activity: Cowboys And Indians, Space Men, and Moon Men

Children divide into two teams and form two parallel lines, thirty to forty feet apart. One line becomes the home of the Cowboys. The other is the home of the Indians. The Cowboys turn their backs while the Indians all clasp hands and move forward in a single line toward the Cowboys. When near enough the teacher calls, "Look out! The Indians are coming!" at which the Cowboys turn around and chase the Indians to their home and tag as many as they can before they reach home. The number of Indians caught is counted and scored. The children return to their own side, and the game continues, with the Indians turning their backs to the Cowboys.

Application:

Children have the opportunity to practice counting the number of children tagged. Team scores can be compared, and the concept of *more Indians* and *less Cowboys* caught can be developed. Children can get the concept of subtraction by seeing how many are caught and how many are left of the total number.

Concept: Quantitative Aspects of Numbers and Counting
Activity: Number Man

One child, the Number Man, faces the class, standing on a line at the end of the play area. Each child in the line is given a number by counting off. The Number Man calls out, "All numbers greater than ———." The children who have numbers greater than the one called must try to get to the other side without being tagged by the Number Man. The Number Man may also call out, "All numbers less than ———." Anyone who is tagged must help the Number Man tag the runners. Any child who runs out of turn is considered tagged.

Application:

The children become more familiar with counting and cardinal concepts through having to decide which numbers are greater than or less than.

Concept: Counting—In Multiples of One's, Two's, Five's
Activity: Count, Move, and Stop

One child is *it*. He stands behind a finish line. All the other children are at a starting line that is drawn twenty-five to fifty feet away, parallel to the finish line. The children sit in a cross-legged sitting position, arms crossed on chests, at the starting line. The child who is *it* hides his eyes and counts to ten (or 20 or 100, depending upon the skills of the group) in any way he chooses, by one's, two's, or five's. While *it* is counting, the players come to a standing position and move toward the finish line during the count. *It* must call the numbers loudly enough for all to hear. At the call of ten (or whatever number has been decided upon), *it* opens his eyes. All players must be seated cross-legged and with arms crossed on chest, at the point to which they have advanced. Any child caught out of position must return to the starting line and begin again. The game continues in this manner until one child has crossed the finished line and is seated before *it* has completed the count. The first child over the line interrupts the count by calling "over." All children return to the starting line, and the game begin again with this child as the new *it*.

Application:

This game provides the necessary repetition of counting by one's, two's, and five's for each child, since not only is *it* counting but each child is counting in order to determine his movement forward.

Concept: Counting—In Multiples of Three's
Activity: Pick-Up Race

A number of wooden blocks (3 or more for each child) are scattered over a large playing area. The children divide into several teams and take their place in rows behind a starting line. At the starting line there are circles drawn, one for each team. On a signal the first child runs into the playing area and picks up one block, returns to the starting line and places a block in his team's circle. He then goes back after a second block and returns it to the circle. He gets the third block and leaves the three blocks in a pile in the circle. Play continues in this manner until each child on the team has collected and piled three blocks in the team's circle. The first team that completes the task wins.

Application:

The children count out how many three's are necessary for each team and how many for all the teams together. Blocks may be counted in groups of three's for those children who have difficulty in identifying the quantity of blocks needed in order for them to see the number of blocks needed.

Concept: Counting—Forward and Backward
Activity: Pass Ball Relay

Children divide into teams. The team members line up one behind the other and close enough so they can easily pass a ball overhead to each other. On a signal a ball is passed over each child's head to the end of the line. As the children pass the ball overhead, they call out the number of their position on the team as one, two, three until the ball reaches the end of the line. When the last child on the team receives the ball, he calls his number and then passes the ball forward again. The next to the last child calls out his number and continues passing the ball forward to the front of the team. For variation the ball may be passed in different ways, for example under the legs, alternating over and under. The winner is the first team to pass the ball forward and back with correct number-counting forwards and backwards.

Application:

Children gain quickness in counting forward and backward in this activity. They are able to get a better understanding of ordinal numbers and their sequence. The teacher may start the counting at any number, depending on the skills of the group.

Concept: Counting—By One's and Ten's
Activity: Bouncing Relay

The children are divided into several teams. The members of each team stand side by side. The first child bounces a playground ball ten times consecutively, calling out the number of each bounce. When he has counted to ten, he passes the ball to the second child. The second child then bounces the ball ten times, calling out the number of each bounce, but on the tenth bounce he calls "twenty." He then passes the ball to the third child. All team members follow the same pattern (1, 2, 3, 4, . . . 9, 30) until each person has bounced the ball and added by tens to reach the proper total. For example, if there are eight children on a team, the last child should end his count with "eighty." At any time a child misses before completing ten bounces, he retrieves the ball and continues his counting. The first team reaching the correct total wins.

Application:

This activity provides practice in counting by one's and ten's. Counting with each bounce helps to develop the understanding of ordinal and cardinal numbers.

Concept: Counting—By Ten's to One Hundred
Activity: Red Light

Two lines are marked off thirty feet apart in a play area. One child is *it*. The child who is *it* stands on one line. The remaining children are grouped at the other line. *It* turns his back to the children and counts loudly "10, 20, 30, 40, . . . 100, Red Light!" The children advance toward him as he counts, but they must stop as he calls "Red Light." As *it* calls "Red Light" he turns, and if he sees anyone moving, he sends the child back to the starting line. The object of the game is to see which child can reach the goal line first.

Application:

This game gives the children the opportunity to practice counting by tens, both *it* and the children, in order for them to know when to stop moving. With each child involved in counting, the activity provides the necessary repetition for all children.

Concept: Number Line
Activity: Number Line Relay

The class is divided into teams of ten. A set of number cards from one to ten is provided for each team. A number line is on the blackboard in front of each team. On a signal the first child on each team selects the number which the teacher calls out from the team's set of cards. When he has found the number from the card set, the child runs up to the team's number line and places it in the proper space on the line. When the number is in place, he then returns, and the child behind him now selects the number from the set of cards which would either follow the first number called *or* come before the number called. Each child on the team proceeds in this manner until all the numbers are correctly placed on the number line. The first team finished wins.

Application:

In this game the children acquire the understanding of number lines and number order and sequence. They can be helped to think of numbers as being equally spaced on the number line.

Concept: Ordinal Numbers
Activity: Leader Ball

Two teams stand in circle formation. On a given signal the leader of each team passes a ball to the player on his right, who passes it to the next player, and so on, until it reaches the leader. The leader calls, "first round" immediately and continues to pass the ball for the "second round" and "third round." At the end of the third round, the leader raises the ball to signify that his team has finished. A point is scored for the team finishing first.

Application:

The time interval in counting by "first round, second round, third round" at the completion of passing the ball around the circle each turn helps to emphasize the ordinal concept of numbers. Children need to keep in mind the number to be called each time.

Concept: Ordinal Numbers
Activity: Fetch And Carry (Rescue Relay)

Two lines are drawn about twenty-five feet apart, one a starting line and the other the goal line. The class is divided into teams of six. With a large group there will be several teams. Each member of the team is assigned a position, for example first, second, through sixth. It might be helpful for some children to have each child, as he stands in line, to call off the ordinal number of his position. In doing this, they can be helped to understand what ordinal numbers mean. The object of the game is for each team to get all its members from the starting line to the goal line. The teams line up at the starting line, facing the goal line. On a signal the first child on each team calls out his ordinal number and takes the hand of the second child and runs with him to the goal line. The first child remains there. The second child runs back to the team, calls out his ordinal number, and takes the hand of the third child on the team. They run to the goal line. Now, the second child remains there while the third child returns to get the fourth team member. This procedure continues until one team wins by getting all of its members across the goal line and in correct order first. (The teacher might walk through the relay procedures with the children so they know what to do. After this practice the game can begin.)

Application:

This acting out of ordinal numbers makes it easier to understand the concept of position and sequence of numbers.

Concept: Ordinal Numbers
Activity: The Number Race

The class is divided into three teams of ten each. Each member of the teams is given a number from one to ten. They line up behind a starting line in correct numerical order. When the teacher gives a signal, the teams race to the finish line and sit down one behind the other in their proper number order and in their proper group. The first team finished scores a point. Number assignments should be frequently changed.

Application:

Children are helped to note which numbers come before and after their number assignments. Changing numbers will help the children to develop greater facility with ordinal numbers.

Concept: Ordinal Numbers

Activity: Call And Catch[5]

The children stand in a circle. The teacher stands in the circle with a rubber ball. Each child is assigned a different number. The teacher throws the ball into the air and calls out a number by saying, "Before six" or "After five." For example, if the teacher calls "After five," the child assigned number six tries to catch the ball after it bounces. The teacher can provide for individual differences of children. For the slower child the teacher can call the number and then momentarily hold the ball before throwing it in the air.

Application:

This activity provides children the opportunity to become familiar with the sequence of ordinal numbers as they practice counting forward and backward.

Concept: Numeral Recognition Beyond One Hundred

Activity: Postman Game

The class is divided into two teams. The members of the first team are the postmen and are given envelopes, each having a house number. Members of the other team represent houses and hold numbers in their hands. Each postman must deliver his envelope to the right address. Each postman runs to the various houses trying to find the correct address. Each postman must be able to read his number aloud. When all the letters have been delivered to the houses, the teams exchange places. The team that delivers the mail in the shortest period of time wins.

Application:

This game is a reinforcement activity to help children to learn to recognize the numerals above one hundred quickly. This game can be varied by using any numerals that the teacher wishes to have the children learn to recognize quickly.

Concept: Roman Numerals

Activity: Roman Numeral Relay

The children are divided into teams. Cards are made for each

---

[5]Humphrey, James H.: Teaching Children Mathematics Through Games, Rhythms, and Stunts. LP No. 5000, Deal, N. J., Kimbo Records, 1968.

team with Roman numerals from I to X (later to XX). The cards are mixed up and placed in a box a specified distance from the starting line for each team. The first child of each team runs to the team box and looks for the Roman numeral for I and returns to his place. The second child then runs to the box to find the Roman numeral for II. This continues until each team member has found the Roman numeral representing his position in line. The first team to find the correct Roman numerals and are standing in place wins.

Concept: Roman Numerals
Activity: Roman Numeral Bounce
The game starts with everyone seated at their desks. The children count one through ten (later 20) until everyone has a number. The teacher then bounces out a number. The children who have that number race to the blackboard to write the Roman numeral for the number of times the ball was bounced. The first one to write the number correctly gets to choose the next Roman numeral and bounce the ball.
Application:
These activities are designed to reinforce previous work with Roman numerals. Children enjoy competing with one another in these game situations, in finding cards, bouncing balls, and writing numbers. In both games the quantitative aspect of each Roman numeral is emphasized.

Addition

Concept: Addition
Activity: Three Deep
The children stand by two's, one behind the other, in a circle. All face the center. A runner and chaser stand outside the circle. The chaser tries to tag the runner. In order to save himself, the runner may run around the circle and stand in front of one of the couples in the circle. This makes the group three deep, and the outside child in the group must now run. He is then chased and tries to save himself in the same way. The outside person in a group of three must always run. If the runner is tagged, he becomes the chaser and must turn and chase the new runner.

Application:

The teacher assists the children in identifying groups of two's when the circle is formed for the game. When a runner stands in front of a group of two, the teacher assists the children to identify that two and one make three.

Concept: Addition

Activity: Back To Back

The children stand back to back with arms interlocked at the elbows. The teacher calls for any size group. On a signal the children let go and must find a new partner if the teacher called for a group of two. Each time the teacher should have the children identify how many children must be added to one in order to make the size group that has been called. If the number called is larger than the group already formed, the teacher may ask how many children are needed to become the size group that has just been called for. Whatever the size group called for, the children must hook up back to back in that number. A time limit may be set. The children who are left over may rejoin the group each time a new set is called.

Application:

In this game the teacher can help the children compare the sizes of the different groups. The teacher can help them act out the number of children to add to one or the existing group in order to form the next group called.

Concept: Addition

Activity: Addition Tag

Each child is given a card bearing a numeral from one to nine which he keeps throughout the game. One child is then chosen to be the tagger. He may go to any child and tag him. The tagger then adds his number to that of the child he tagged. If the sum is correct, the child who was tagged becomes the tagger, and so on.

Application:

Such a game provides practice in adding for those who need it most, the child who does not know, or makes a mistake, as there is no penalty by having to drop out of the game. For children who score perfectly for several days, it should be arranged for some other enrichment work or games while the others are playing this game.

Concept: Addition

Activity: Beanbag Throw (Variation)

Five large-mouth cans are tied together and are numbered from one to five. The class is divided into teams. A set of cans is required for each team. The teams stand in rows behind a line about ten feet from the targets. Each team member throws a beanbag, trying to get it in the number five can, as this is worth the most points. Each child has three tries. At the end of his turn, each child adds up his own score, and it is recorded for his team. When all the children have had their turns, they add the scores to find which team has the most points. This team wins. In case of a tie, there is a play off.

Application:

A game of this type stimulates interest in arithmetic drill. This game may be played with higher numbers as the children progress. Children who are having difficulty in adding may be helped by the teacher to count out their scores.

Concept: Addition

Activity: Add-A-Number Relay

Divide the class into several teams. Place as many numbers as there are teams on the blackboard. (Use low, one-digit numbers at first.) The teacher writes or calls out a number. The first team member of each team runs to the board and adds this number to his team's number on the board. He returns to his team, and the next team member runs to the board and adds the same number to the new sum. Each child on the team does the same until the first team who is finished wins. Each team should start with different numbers to prevent copying. Size of numbers used will depend on the developmental level of the children.

Application:

This game provides reinforcement of addition facts that are presented visually. There can be wide variation in the difficulty of the addition facts used, depending on the individual children. This same activity can be used for subtraction facts and is called Subtract-A-Number Relay.

Concept: Addition (1-10)

Activity: Beanbag Toss

A board is made three or four feet square with a small eight-inch circle cut out in the center of the square. A child standing ten feet from the board tosses five beanbags, one at a time, at the board. If he hits the square, he scores one point and three points if the beanbag goes through the hole in the center. The child may total his score and record it. The child with the highest score wins.

Application:

This activity enables children to use their addition facts in an exciting and highly motivating situation in their totaling of their scores.

Concept: Addition (1-10)

Activity: Number Catch

Every child is given a number from one to ten. The teacher calls "two plus two" or "six plus one" and tosses the ball into the air. Any child whose number happens to be the sum of the numbers called can catch the ball. The other children run away as fast as they can until the child catches the ball and calls "Stop." At that time all the children must stop where they are and remain standing in place. The child with the ball may take three long, running strides in any direction toward the children. He then throws the ball, trying to hit one of the children. If he succeeds, the child who is hit has one point scored against him. The game continues, with the teacher calling out another addition problem. The children with the lowest number of points are the winners.

Application: (Follows this section of activities for reinforcement of addition facts inasmuch as the application is the same.)

Concept: Addition (1-10)

Activity: Steal The Bacon (Variation)

The class is divided into equal teams, and each member is given a number. The teams line up some twenty or twentiy-five feet apart, with any object at the center equidistant from both teams. The children on each team should be mixed up so they are *not* numerically lined up in correct ordinal sequence. The regular game of Steal the Bacon is played except that the teacher calls out a simple addition problem, and the child from each team whose assigned number is the answer to the problem must try to steal the bacon first in order to score a point for his team.

Application: (Follows this section of activities for reinforcement of addition facts.)

Concept: Addition (1-10)
Activity: Space Demon

There are twenty-one children with ten on each team and a Space Demon. The two teams line up facing each other about twenty feet apart. The distance between the two teams represents *space*. Each team counts off so each member is assigned a number. The teacher calls out an addition problem whose sum will not be greater than ten. The children representing the parts of the problem (the addends), as well as the children representing the answer of sum from each team, try to exchange places before the Space Demon tags one of them. If a child is tagged, his team gets one point. The team with the lowest score within a set time wins.

Application: (Follows this section of activities for reinforcement of addition facts.)

Concept: Addition (1-10)
Activity: Number Man (Variation)

Each child is assigned a number and stands behind a line at one end of the play area. One child, the Number Man, calls out various addition problems. The children who have the number that answers the problem must try to get past the Number Man to the line on the opposite side without being tagged. If tagged, the child must help the Number Man. The teacher may reassign numbers frequently and have children change places with the Number Man.

Application: (Follows this section of activities for reinforcement of addition facts.)

Concept: Addition (1-10)
Activity: Arithmetic Relay

Children may be divided into several teams of equal numbers.

The teams stand in rows about twenty feet from a blackboard. The teacher calls out a fact, and the first person on each team, runs to the blackboard and writes down the answer. One point is given to the team who writes down the correct answer first. The game may be played using running, walking, hopping on right foot, hopping on left foot, skipping, and jumping with both feet. The teacher may also find it desirable to have the children write the problem on the board in addition to giving the answer. She may have the children write the number problem in the several ways they have learned to express a number sentence. The team with the highest score wins.

Application:

These activities presenting addition facts in the manner of game-type situations provide the repetition and reinforcement needed by children to develop the skills involved. Children need to become so familiar with the basic number facts that they can respond quickly when using them in more complex mathematics problems. These highly motivating, active games help to develop these skills and to maintain them.

The teacher can provide for individual differences of children in the playing of these games. When necessary, children may act out those facts giving them difficulty, for example three children plus two children are counted and found equal to five children. For the slower child the teacher can plan to control the situation in such a way as to provide him more time to respond to the task. This can be done, for example, when the teacher calls the number and then momentarily holds the ball before throwing it in the air. This enables the slower child to have additional time to think out the answer.

These games may also be used with the addition of larger numbers as the teacher considers it appropriate. These games can also be adapted to develop subtraction, multiplication, and division skills.

Concept: Addition—Word Symbols in a Number Sentence
Activity: Lions And The Hunters

Two teams are established. One team, the hunters, begins by forming a large circle. The other team (lions) are in the circle.

The hunters use a ball as a bullet and attempt to hit (shoot) as many lions as possible within a two-minute period. As the lions are hit, they go to a lion cage for the hunter team that has been marked in chalk on the court. When the teams change places, the second group of lions shot go to a second lion cage marked on the court. A scorer records the number of lions shot by each hunter team. The cages are marked in chalk along with the other symbols in the number sentence.

cage		cage		
2	**+**	*5*	**=**	*7*
	plus		equals	
addend		addend		sum

Application:

The lions shot by each team supply the numbers in the cages. The children may count the lions in the cages. They must then add the number of lions in the cages (the addends) in order to find how many lions were shot altogether (sum). The teacher should also question children regarding the names and meanings of *plus* and *equal*.

Concept: Addition—Place Value of One's, Ten's, and One Hundred's

Activity: Bundle Relay

The class is divided into two teams. Toothpicks, pencils, popsicle sticks, or any other appropriate items are grouped into bundles of one's, ten's, and one hundred's. The teacher announces a number, as seventy-two. Each team must figure how many bundles of ten's and one's are necessary to arrive at the number called. The object of the game is for each member of a team to pick up *one* bundle (1's, 10's 100's) until the total number of items in the bundles equals the number called. The first child runs from the starting line and picks up one bundle of ten's and brings it back to the team. The second child runs and gets one bundle of ten's. This procedure is followed until the seventh child gets the last bundle of ten's needed. The eight and ninth child then run and get one bundle of one's in order to have their items equal seventy-two. The first team with the proper number of bundles and the correct total gets one point. It is important for the children to understand they may pick up only one bundle, regardless of size, at a time. For the next number called by the teacher, the child who would be next in line starts the running to get the number of bundles decided upon by the team.

Application:

The children learn to evaluate a given number in terms of the number of one's, ten's, and one hundred's in that number. They have the opportunity to use their understanding of this concept of numbers in an interesting and highly motivating activity.

Concept: Addition—Place value With Zero as a Place Holder
Activity: Place Value Relay

The children are divided into two teams called Black Team and White Team. Each child is given a large card which has a numeral painted on it. The numerals used are from zero to nine. The children in the Black Team have black cards with white numerals; the White Team has white cards with black numerals. Each team should have three or four children who have cards with zero painted on them. The teacher calls a number containing any grouping of numerals desired, such as 5,004. The children in both teams holding the numeral 5, 0, 0, and 4 run to the front of the room and place themselves correctly to form the number. The first team to get into position gets a point. The team that scores fifteen points first wins the game.

Application:

This game is helpful in teaching children to read and write the larger numbers. The children have learned that numbers have place values. In using this game, emphasis should be given to the fact that the position of individual numbers makes an important difference in the value of the complete number. For those having difficulty seeing this, bundles of one's, ten's, and one hundred's might be available to demonstrate the quantitative differences of misplaced numbers.

Subtraction

Concept: Subtraction

Activity: Ten Little Birds

The children form a circle. Ten children are selected for the birds, and they count off from one to ten. They go into the center of the circle and stand in a line within the circle. When the verses are sung, the child in the center with the number being repeated "flies" back to his original position in the circle formed by the children. This is repeated until all the birds have moved back to the circle with the other children. The song may be sung again with other children selected to be birds.

Ten little birdies sitting on a line,
One flew away and then there were nine.

Nine little birdies sitting up straight,
One fell down and then there were eight.

Eight little birdies looking up to heaven,
One went away and then there were seven.

Seven little birdies picking up sticks,
One flew away and then there were six.

Six little birdies sitting on a hive,
One got stung and then there were five.

Five little birdies peeping through a door,
One went in and then there were four.

Four little birdies sitting in a tree,
One fell down and then there were three.

Three little birdies looking straight at you,
One went away and then there were two.

Two little birdies sitting in the sun,
One went home and then there was one.

One little birdie left all alone,
He flew away and then there was none.

Application:

In this rhythmic activity, children are able to act out the

concept of subtraction. The children can understand more readily by seeing the group grow smaller each time one is taken away.

Concept: Subtraction
Activity: Take Away, Take Away[6]

The children stand in a circle. One child is *it*. He walks around inside the circle. As the children sing the following song (to the tune of "Twinkle Twinkle Little Star,") they act out the words of the song.

> Take away, take away, take away one.
> Come with me and have some fun.
> Take away, take away, take away two.
> Come with me, oh yes please do.
> Take away, take away, take away three.
> All please come and skip with me.

It taps one child. This child follows behind *it*. *It* then taps a second and a third child. At the end of the song all three children try to get back to their places in the circle. *It* also tries to get into one of the vacant places. The remaining child becomes *it* for the next game.

Application:

This singing game enables children to see demonstrated the concept of subtraction. The teacher may have the children identify how many children are left each time *it* takes away one child.

Concept: Subtraction
Activity: Musical Chairs

Any given number of children form a circle with one less chair than there are children. As the music plays, children walk, run, hop, or skip around the chairs until the music stops. At this time all children try to find a seat. The extra child is then *out*. Out takes a chair with him. The music starts again, and the class repeats as above. The teacher may take out two or three chairs at a time.

Application:

The teacher helps the children to note that *take away*, as in the case of taking the chair from the circle, is subtraction. There

---

[6]Humphrey, James H.: *Ibid.*

is subtraction by one if one chair is taken away or subtraction by two or three if two or three chairs are taken away.

Concept: Subtraction
Activity: Ten Little Chickadees
　Groups of ten children form lines, facing forward. The children in each line count off one to ten, from left to right. As the verses are sung, the child with that number sits down.

> Ten little chickadees standing in a line,
> One flew away, now there're nine.

> Nine little chickadees standing very straight,
> One flew away, now there're eight.

> Eight little chickadees looking up to heaven,
> One flew away, now there're seven.

> Seven little chickadees build a nest of sticks,
> One flew away, now there're six.

> Six little chickadees looking very alive,
> One flew away, now there're five.

> Five little chickadees pecking at my door,
> One flew away, now there're four.

> Four little chickadees very afraid of me,
> One flew away, now there're three.

> Three little chickadees didn't know what to do,
> One flew away, now there're two.

> Two little chickadees look toward the sun,
> One flew away, now there're one.

> One little chickadee hopping on the ground,
> He flew away, now there're none around.

Application:
　Children are able to visualize the subtraction process in this rhythmic activity. The teacher may stop the song at any point and have the children identify the subtraction fact appropriate

for that particular verse. After the song the teacher might have the children write the different number sentences.

Concept: Subtraction
Activity: Dodge Ball

The class is divided into two teams. One team forms a circle, and the second team stands inside the circle. The regular game of Dodge Ball is played. Players outside the circle try to hit the team in the center with a volley ball by throwing it rapidly. The children in the center, to avoid being hit, may move about, jump, stoop, but they may not leave the circle. The team on the outside may throw the ball only from the circle. When a child in the center is hit, he leaves the circle. Each time a child is hit, the outside team should call out "ten minus one equals nine." The team with the largest number of children still in the center at the end of two minutes wins the game.

Application:

Children can apply the concept that subtraction is the operation of taking objects from a group and finding the remainder by counting the number of players eliminated from each team whenever a child is hit and at the end of the game.

Concept: Subtraction
Activity: Animal Catch

Two parallel lines about twenty feet apart are marked off. One child, the Animal Catcher, stands in the center area between the two lines. On one of the lines the other children form in groups of four (or 5, 6, and so on) facing the Animal Catcher. Each group selects the name of an animal such as Bear, Elephant, Camel, or Tiger. The Animal Catcher calls the name of one group of animals. These children try to run to the opposite line without being tagged by the Animal Catcher. If so, they remain as animals. Those children who are caught help the Animal Catcher to tag members of the other animal groups when called.

Application:

The teacher helps the children to identify groups of four or whatever size group is selected. At intervals during the game the teacher has the opportunity to develop the meaning of subtraction by asking such questions as "How many horses were caught?," "How many did we start with?," and "How many horses are left?" Children can be helped to count out the answers if necessary.

Concept: Subtraction
Activity: Cheese and Mice
    A round mousetrap is formed by the children standing in a circle. In the center of the mousetrap is placed the cheese (a ball or some other object). The children are each assigned numbers (zero, 1, 2, up to 10). Several children can be assigned to each number. When the teacher calls a number from zero to ten, all the children with the number that represents the difference or remainder of the number called from ten leave their places in the circle, run around the outside of the circle, and then return to their original places (hole in the trap). They then run into the circle to get the cheese. The first child who gets the cheese is the winning mouse. The teacher must check to see that the children with the correct number for the answer to the problem were the mice who ran to get the cheese. Only a child who was the correct number can win.

Application:
    In this activity the children are provided opportunity for drill in subtraction facts whose difference is less than ten. Speed and accuracy can be developed. The teacher may assign other numbers and call out more difficult problems according to the skills of the group. This game could be adapted to addition, multiplication, and division.

Concept: Subtraction
Activity: Tossing Darts
    Two circles are drawn on a chalkboard. A line is drawn at a distance from the board. (The teacher must adjust the size of the circles and the distance for throwing to accommodate individuals.) Two relay teams are counted off. Running to the line, a child from Team A throws from five to ten safety suction-type darts at the first circle. A child from Team B throws the same number of darts at the second circle. The object of the game is to cancel the score of the child with the higher score by taking away the

score of the child with the lower score. Whichever team had the higher score gets the remainder as the score. The second child from each team proceeds in the same manner. The team with the higher score wins.

Application:

Children can apply subtraction principles by removing one dart in the first circle for each dart removed from the second circle. The remaining darts in the circle with the most darts are the number left (difference). The teacher might want to write the number sentence on the board, showing the subtraction problem.

$$6 - 2 = 4$$

Multiplication

Concept: Multiplication
Activity: Call Ball (Variation)

The children stand in a circle. The teacher stands in the center of the circle with a ball. The teacher calls out a combination (7 x 7). The teacher then bounces the ball to a child in the circle, and he must try to catch the ball and give the correct answer before the teacher counts to ten. One point is given for knowing the fact, another for catching the ball. The teacher may elect to have a child be the one in the center calling the problems and bouncing the ball. In such a case, it should be emphasized that all children should be given a chance to catch the ball and give an answer to a problem.

Application:

This game is a little easier for children to play than the regular game of Call Ball, where they have to be very quick to remember the answer to a given problem. This activity helps to provide the necessary repetition to build skills in the multiplication facts. Addition, subtraction, and division facts might also be used for this game.

Concept: Multiplication by Two's
Activity: Twice As Many

The children stand on a line near the end of the play area and face the caller. The caller stands at the finish line some twenty-five to fifty feet away and gives directions as "Take two hops. Now take twice as many. Take three small steps. Now take twice as many." Directions are varied in number and type of movement. Each direction is following by "now take twice as many." The first child to reach the finish line calls out "twice as many," and everyone runs back to the starting line. The caller tags all those he can before they reach the starting line. All those tagged help the caller the next time.

Application:

Children are able to apply their *multiplication-by-two* facts to a highly motivating activity. The teacher may check each time a new direction is given to be sure the children have multiplied by two accurately and have the correct answer. This activity encourages children to respond quickly to the multiplication facts. Those children who are having difficulty may be helped by the teacher to act out the multiplication fact called for.

Concept: Multiplication by Two's

Activity: Grand March

A leader is chosen, and all the children line up behind him and march around the room to marching or walking music. The following pattern is used in marching:

1. March in a circle single file.

2. Follow the leader up the center in single file.

3. The first child goes off to the right, and the second goes off to the left. (Continue with the children going alternately to the right and to the left.)

4. The two new leaders circle and meet at the back of the marching area and come forward as a couple. (All children pair off in the same manner.)

5. The couples come up the center, the first couple goes off to the right, and the second couple goes off to the left. (Continue with partners going alternately to the right and to the left.)

6. The couples circle and meet at the back and form rows of four each.

7. Rows of four come up the center and go off in alternating directions.

8. Rows circle and meet, forming rows of eight, and so on.

9. Continue in this manner until all children come forward in a straight line.

Application:

When the formation is explained, the children might figure out how many children can be used. They could walk through and check their figures. The children, knowing the total number in their class, might figure out how many times they will circle before all the children are joined in rows of two, four, eight, sixteen, and so on. They could figure out how many sets of two, four, and so on and what division fact is represented by each formation.

Division

Concept: Division
Activity: Triplet Tag

The children form groups of three, with hands joined. As the groups are formed, the teacher should point out that the total number of children to be divided is the *dividend,* the group size of three children is the *divisor,* and the resulting number of groups is the *quotient.* If the whole group cannot be divided equally, the children will see that there are some left over, or the *remainder.* The groups stand scattered about the play area. One group is *it* and carries a red cloth. The *it* group tries to tag another group of three. Hands must be joined at all times. When a group is tagged, it is given the red cloth, and the game continues.

Application:

The children have the opportunity to act out the division process in this game. The children can readily see the quotient by counting the groups.

Concept: Division—The Effect of Decreasing or Increasing the Divisor on the Quotient When the Dividend Remains the Same

Activity: Birds Fly South

Play begins with the entire class distributed randomly behind a starting line. The entire class represents the dividend. A caller gives the signal to play by calling "Birds fly south in flocks of six" (or the highest number that will be used to divide the number, the divisor.) The class runs to another line that has been designated as *South*. At this point the children should be grouped in sixes. After observing the number of flocks (the quotient), the remainders become *hawks*, who take their places between the two lines. Then with the call "Scatter! The hawks are coming!" the children run back to the other line, with the hawks attempting to tag them. Note is taken of who is tagged. Play continues, with the entire class taking its place behind the starting line. The caller then uses the next lowest number for the call. If six was used first, five would be called next. "Birds fly south in flocks of five." This continues until the smallest group can be made which would be two. Each time the children should observe the number of flocks (the quotient).

To score the game, each child would begin with a score equivalent to the number which is called first, for example, in this case, the number six. If he is tagged, his score increases by one point.

Application:

At the end of the game the class should evaluate the arithmetic learning involved by noting that when the total number of children remained the same (dividend) and the size of the flocks (divisor) decrease, then the number of flocks (quotient) increased. After this pattern has been established, the numbers called can be reversed, beginning with the smallest divisor and working up to the highest divisor to be used. Here, the converse of the previous understanding can be developed.

Concept: Division—The Effect of Decreasing or Increasing the Divident on the Quotient When the Divisor Remains the Same

Activity: Birds Fly South (Variation)

Starting with the entire class on the starting line, at the signal "Birds fly south in flocks of six" (or the highest number that would be used to divide the number), the class runs to the line designated as *South*. At this point they should group by sixes or whatever the divisor. After observing the quotient in terms of the number of *flocks*, the remainders become *hawks*, who take their place between the two lines. Then, with the call "Scatter, the hawks are coming!" the children ungroup and run back to the other line, with the hawks attempting to tag them. All children caught, and hawks retire to a *hawks nest*. A point is scored by the individuals left when the total can no longer be divided into the groups originally established as the divisor.

Application:

The change in total number of children at the starting line (dividend) each time is noted, and play continues in like manner, with emphasis put on the number of flocks or groups that is the outcome when the dividend has been reduced.

Concept: Division—Averages
Activity: Beanbag Throw

Two parallel lines five to ten feet in length are marked approximately fifty to eighty feet apart, depending on the group. The children are divided into two groups; each group is assigned to a line. One child from the first group is given a beanbag. The game is begun by the child with the beanbag, tossing it from behind the starting line. One child from the opposite side then marks the spot where the beanbag landed, while another child measures the distance with a tape measure. A scorekeeper records the distance. The second group is now allowed to throw a beanbag from their starting line. It is now marked, measured, and recorded by members of the first team. Play continues until all children have had three throws. The child with the longest average distance is the winner.

Application:

The class records the distance of each child's throw. By having to add and divide their own distances, the children learn what an average is and how to find an average. This activity also provides opportunity to practice measuring distance and to use basic processes of addition and division.

Fractions

Concept: Fractions—Numerator and Denominator
Activity: Corner Spry

In a rectangular playing area a circle about ten feet in diameter is marked in the center. There are four equal teams, and a captain for each team is chosen. One team is in each corner of the playing area while the four captains take their places inside the circle. Each captain has a ball. There is a caller assigned; there may be a scorer. Each team member represents one part of the total number on the team, for example he may represent one-third, one-fourth, or one-eighth of the team.

The caller calls different fractions (involving thirds, fourth, or eights, depending on the total number of children on the teams) in any order. When the caller calls a fraction, that number of each team must squat. The captain of each team will then pass and receive the ball, with each of his team remaining standing. The first one finished with this exchange without dropping the ball scores a point, and another fraction is called.

Application:

Children should be helped to note that the number of children who squat (numerator) represent the number of parts of the total number of units (denominator) being used.

Concept: Fractions—As a Ratio or Relationship Between Numbers

Activity: Hit Or Miss

Children are divided into teams. Each team is given an eraser, which is set on a table, chalk tray, or the floor. The teams stand in rows a specified distance from the erasers. Each child is given three or four erasers. He tosses the erasers trying to knock down the one set up on the table. As each child plays, he calls out his scores, expressing it as a fraction. One hit in four tries equals one-fourth; three-fourth would represent three hits in four attempts, and so on. The team with the highest score wins.

Application:

Children can learn to use the relationship between successful and unsuccessful attempts at making points to build meaning of fractions. The children can use this concept in those situations in which they are practicing skills such as shooting baskets or any other type of throw for accuracy.

Concept: Fractions

Activity: Flannelboard Fractions

The children are divided into teams. Flannelboards are set up, one for each team. About fifteen feet away each team stands in a row and is given a fraction kit prepared for sticking to the flannel-board. On a given signal the teacher calls out a fraction. The first child of each team selects the correct fractional part from the team kit, runs, places the fractional part on the board, and returns to his team. The first child to do this scores a point for his team. The teacher then calls out another fraction, and the second child of each team proceeds in the same manner. The team with the highest score wins. For a variation the teacher can hold up a card with the fraction for the children to find in the fraction kit.

Application:

In this activity children have the opportunity to handle and to develop their recognition of various fraction parts. The teacher can help children find the fraction called for by using the fraction kit and working out the proper identification of the fraction by comparing the various fraction parts.

Concept: Fractions

Activity: End Ball

A play area twenty-five by fifty feet is marked off. The area is then divided by lines so that four lines (including the end lines) are equidistant from each other about twelve feet apart. The class is divided into two teams. Each team is again divided into two groups. The groups from each team take places along the four lines so that they alternate with the groups of the other team. The object of the game is for each team to try to throw the ball over the heads of the opposing team. Points are scored when the ball is caught by the opposing team as it is thrown over their heads. The team with the highest score within a given time limit wins.

Application:

The children are helped to find one-half of the class to make up the two teams. They then find one-half of each team to form the two groups within each team. It can be brought out that each group represents one-fourth of the total class number. It can also be brought out that to divide the class into fourths, the total number of the class could have been divided by four. Children can then be encouraged to find other parts, divisions, or fractions of other size groups.

Concept: Fractions—Halves, Fourths, Eighths
Activity: Fraction Target Relay

A diagram may be drawn (circle, square, rectangle) on the play area. The diagram is then marked with one-half, one-quarter, and two-eighths. A throwing line is drawn ten or fifteen feet from the diagram. Teams are formed. Each child on a team gets to throw three beanbags at the diagram. In scoring, each fractional part is worth a different score. The one-half section is equal to four points, one-fourth is two points, and one-eighth is one point. The scorekeeper for each team totals the individual scores. The team with the lowest score wins.

Application:

In introducing this game, attention is called to the fact the different fractions have varying point values, that one-half is equal to four-eighths so they can make four points when the beanbag hits the fractional part one-half, and so on. This game also helps the children to visualize the relationship of the fractions in terms of size.

Concept: Addition of Fractions
Activity: Hit The Target

The class is divided into teams. Each team has a beanbag and a target area drawn on the play area. The target area should be about a five feet square with five circles (each 10 inches in diameter) drawn in the square and marked with different fractions, all with the same denominator. There should be a scorer for each team. The first players on each team throw a beanbag at the teams' targets. Each team scores the fraction within the circle that is hit. After each child has had a turn, the scorekeepers add the fractions, and the team with the highest score wins.

Application:

In this type of activity, children have the opportunity to add fractions with a common denominator in a highly motivating situation. Each child on the teams should be encouraged to check the scorekeeper.

Concept: Subtraction of Fractions
Activity: Train Dodge

The class forms a circle with four children in the center. The children in the center hold each other about the waist, thus making a train. The object of the game is to tag the *Caboose,* or last child. One or more dodge balls may be used to try to hit the Caboose. As the Caboose is hit, he can wait outside the circle. The game continues until all four children of the train have been hit. At the outset the teacher establishes the concept that the four children within the circle make up the *whole* train, that each child is one part, one-fourth of the whole train. As each child is hit and moves to the outside of the circle, a brief pause is taken to ascertain that one-fourth of the train is now uncoupled and waiting outside and three-fourths of the cars remain coupled together and in the game. When the next child is hit, two-fourths are in and two-fourths are out. Finally, the whole train is assembled outside the ring and is now in the roundhouse. A new train is then formed with another group of four children.

Application:

This game provides a dramatic means of presenting subtraction of fractions. Midway through the game, the teacher might help the children to note that two-fourths are one-half the train and that an equal number of cars are inside and outside the circle.

Concept: Fractions

Activity: Fraction Race

The class is divided into a number of teams. The members of each team take a sitting position, one behind the other a specified distance from a goal line. Starting with the first child on the teams, the children are assigned numbers, starting with number one. The teacher calls out a fraction of a number. The children whose number is the answer stand, and run to the goal line and return to their original sitting position. If the teacher calls out "one-fourth of eight," all the number two's would run. Similarly, if the teacher calls "one-third of fifteen," all the number five's would run. The first child back scores five points for his team, the second child back scores three points, and the last child scores one point.

Application:

In this game the children are called upon to develop quickness in working out fractions of whole numbers. When necessary, children can work out their problem by counting to help them see the answer.

Decimals

Concept: Decimals
Activity: Roving Decimal Point

Children line up in teams with about five children to a team. a team captain stands in front of each team, ready to record scores. A ball, representing the decimal point, is given to the first child on each team. On a given signal the ball is bounced or passed from child to child up the line and then back again. When the stop signal is given, the decimal point (the ball) stops and is put to the left of the child last holding the ball. Each child then has to tell what place (fraction denominator) he represents. A point is given for each correct answer. If the ball is dropped, it must be taken to the first child on the team and started down the line again.

When everyone has learned the value of each place to the right of the decimal point, the children might be assigned numbers, and the game proceeds as before except this time the captain is required to read the decimal number they represent in order to score. The captain can join the line, and the last child becomes captain after each scoring until each has a turn at being captain. The team having the highest scores wins.

Application:

This game can be used in developing understanding and skill in reading decimal numbers.

Concept: Decimals
Activity: Dash Relay

A 25-yard course is marked off on the playground. The children are grouped into several teams. At a signal to "Go!" the first child on each team runs from the starting line to the finish line. A timer for each team records the running time with a stop watch. Children place their time on a team chart. Running times are recorded in decimal form, for example 5.8 seconds. When each child on the teams has run, the total times are added. The team with the lowest running time wins. The course may be run as often as possible over several weeks as teams try to improve their time.

Application:

In an interesting and highly motivating situation, children have the opportunity to work with decimals. Teams can check their improvement by subtracting. Teams can compare their time with that of the other teams by subtracting. Teams can average their own running time by adding and dividing.

Measurement

Concept: Linear Measurement—Inches, Feet, Yards
Activity: Ring Toss

A regular *ring toss* game can be used for this activity. A yardstick is needed. The class is divided into two teams. Each team has a ring, and one post is used for both teams. The first child on each team takes a turn tossing his ring. Each child then takes the yardstick and measures the distance between the post and his ring. The child's ring closest to the post scores one point for his team. Children should use feet, inches, one-half inches, and one-quarter inches only. The team with the highest score wins.

Application:

Each child has the opportunity to develop his measuring skills to determine the closeness of his ring to the post. He can also check the opposing team member's ring to get additional practice.

Concept: Linear Measurement
Activity: Add-A-Jump Relay

Teams line up in a single-line formation. The first child of each team moves up to a starting line in front of his team and jumps as far as he can. This distance is marked. The second child walks to this mark and jumps as far as he can. The game continues until each child on the team has jumped. The team covering the greatest distance is declared the winner.

Application:

When children are working with linear measures, this relay helps them to be able to measure distances and to gain understanding of how to add, subtract, and compare distance. After each child has had his turn, he can measure the distance of his jump and record it in feet and inches. Children can be assigned to measure the total distance jumped by each team. When the children return to the classroom, they can use these figures to find the average distance jumped, to compare team or individual records, and to add individual distances together and check totals with the recorded team distance. Practice with changing measures to small or larger units is provided.

Concept: Liquid Measurement—Pints and Quarts
Activity: Milkman Tag

Two teams of three milkmen are selected and given milk-truck bases (a tree for instance). One team might be called Chocolate, the other White. The remaining children are called Pints. On a given signal one milkman from each team tries to tag any one of the Pints. When he tags one, they both go to the *milk truck,* and another milkman goes after a Pint. A goal may be set as to the number of Pints needed for a team to win. The teacher can set a goal of so many quarts to be gained in order to win. The children must then figure out how many Pints will be needed to make the necessary number of quarts. They may multiply the number of quarts by two, or they may pair off the Pints and add to determine the number needed for the specified number of quarts.

Application:

Children are provided a highly motivating activity to work with pints and quarts and their equivalents. Children can count the number of Pints caught by each team and group them to figure out if they have the correct number of quarts.

Concept: Telling Time
Activity: Tick Tock

The class forms a circle that represents a clock. Two children are runners and are called Hour and Minute. The children chant "What time is it?" Minute then chooses the hour and calls it out (6 o'clock). Hour and Minute must stand still while the children in the circle call "one o'clock, two o'clock, three o'clock . . . six o'clock" (or whatever time has been chosen). When the children get to the chosen hour, the chase begins. Hour chases Minute clockwise around the outside of the circle. If Hour can catch

Minute before the children in the circle once again call out "one o'clock, two o'clock . . . six o'clock" (the same hour as counted the first time), he chooses another child to become Hour. The game can also be played counting by half-hours.

Application:

Children not only get practice in calling the hours but also develop an understanding of the concept of the term *clockwise.*

Concept: Telling Time

Activity: Set The Clock Relay

Clock faces are drawn on pieces of heavy tagboard. Movable hands are attached to each clock face. The clocks are secured to a bulletin board or a blackboard. Children form two teams in relay formation about ten feet from the clock faces. The teacher calls out an hour such as "seven o'clock." The first child on each team runs, skips, or hops (as directed) to his team's clock and places the hands at seven o'clock. The teacher calls another time, and the second child of each team sets the hands of the clock for that particular time. Each child proceeds until everyone on each team has had a chance to set the clock. For each hour called out, the child who sets the clock first and accurately scores a point for his team. The team with the most points wins.

Application:

Children get the repetition necessary for developing skill in telling time. They not only have their own turn at setting the clock but they should be encouraged to watch the other children to be sure they are not making mistakes.

Concept: Telling Time

Activity: Five Minute Relay

The class is divided into two teams. A cardboard clock with movable hands is set up for each team at the front of the room. The clocks are set for any given time. Each clock may be set at a different time so the teams cannot copy each other. The teams line up in relay formation a specified distance from the clocks. On a signal the first child on each team begins the game by running forward and moves the minute hand ahead by five minutes and writes down the new time on the board. As soon as this child is past the first child on his team when he moves forward to the clock, the team moves back, leaving a space for the first child up at the front of the team's line. As soon as the first child returns, he raises his hand, and the last child on the team proceeds. He moves the minute hand ahead five minues and writes down the time. The first team whose runners all finish setting the clock and writing down the time correctly wins.

Application:

In this activity the children are provided the repetition necessary for learning to tell time quickly and accurately. This game helps to reinforce the skills previously presented in situations that are highly motivating.

Concept: Telling Time
Activity: Clock Race

The class is arranged into teams, as in other relay games. The teacher prepares slips of paper containing statements related to time, such as "Recess begins at 10:40," "The buses leave at 3:15," or "The Flintstone Show begins at 4:00." These statements are placed in a smaller container in front of each team, and clock faces with movable hands are placed on the blackboard ledge. Captains are appointed for each team. At a given signal the captains draw the statements from the containers and read them. The first child on each team runs and sets the team's clock to the specified time in the statement for that team. The child then returns to the team. The captain reads another statement, and the second child on the team then sets the team's clock accordingly. The game continues until one team makes all the clock settings as required. However, if an error occurs, the captain is responsible for detecting it and must correct it before *his* team can proceed to the next statement. The teacher helps to keep track of any errors. The first team finished wins.

Application:

This highly interesting activity provides children a meaningful opportunity for practice in telling time.

Geometry

Concept: The Shortest Distance Between Two Points Is a Straight Line

Activity: Straight-Crooked Relay

The class is divided into four teams. In the relay have one team run directly between two points while the second team has an additional place to tag between the two points that is not in direct line with the other points. Teams should be switched so they alternate, having to run the crooked route.

Application:

The children can note it takes less time to move between two points by following a straight line than by a crooked line because it is the shortest distance. The children can measure the distance of the straight and crooked lines between the two points that are equidistant for the two teams. To account for individual differences of children, the teacher might make sure that both slow and fast runners are assigned to each team.

Concept: The Meaning of Perimeter

Concept: The Shortest Distance Between Two Points Is a Straight Line

Activity: Around The Horn

A small playing field is set up similar to a baseball diamond with a home plate and three bases. The team in the field has a catcher on homeplate and two fielders on each of the bases. The runners of other team stand at home plate. The catcher has the ball. The object of the game is for the catcher and fielders, upon a signal, to relay the ball around the bases and back to home plate *twice* before the runner at home plate can run around and tag each base and proceed to home plate *once*. At the bases the fielders take turns. One takes the first throw, the other the second. The team up to the plate scores a point if it reaches home plate before the ball.

Application:

The distance around the bases is described as the perimeter of the field. Each runner is told he must run the perimeter of the field, and the team in the field is told that the ball must go twice around the perimeter of the field. The children learn that a wild throw which is not in a straight line to the other player takes longer to get to the next base.

Concept:　A Circle Is a Simple Closed Curve Surrounding a Closed
Region

Activity:　Run Circle Run

The class forms a circle by holding hands and facing inward.
Depending on the size of the group, the children count off by two's
or three's (for small groups) or four's, five's, or six's (for large
groups around 30). The teacher calls one of the assigned numbers. All the children with that number start running around
the circle; each runner tries to tag one or more children running
ahead of him. As successful runners reach their starting point
without being tagged, they stop. Runners who are tagged go to
the center of the circle. Another number is called, and the same
procedure is followed. Continue until all have been called. Re-
form the circle, assign new numbers to the children, and repeat.
As the number of children decreases, a circle may be drawn on
the ground which they must stay out of when running around the
circle to their places.

Application:

The children should be helped to note that when they form a
circle by holding hands, they make a continuous, simple, closed
curve. As they play the game, they should observe what happens
when segments break off. They also see how the curve surrounds
a region because the children who are standing in the center
represent points in space within the region.

Concept: Perimeter of a Circle

Activity: Three Bounce Relay

Teams are formed and make rows behind a starting line. A
small circle about one foot in diameter is drawn fifteen feet in
front of the starting line before each team. At a signal the first
child on each team runs with a ball to the circle. At the circle he
attempts to bounce the ball three times within the perimeter of
the circle. If the ball, at any time, does not land within the
perimeter of the circle, the child must start over from the starting
line. When a child has bounced the ball successfully within the
circle, he returns to the starting line, touches the next child, who
does the same thing. The first team finished wins.

Application:

The word *perimeter* is stressed in explaining the game. The children can thus learn the meaning of this term by practical use. Other geometric shapes might be drawn instead of the circle. In this way the concept of *perimeter* can be extended.

Concept: Parallel Lines and Right Angles
Activity: Streets And Alleys

The children divide into three or more parallel lines with at least three feet between children in each direction. A runner and chaser are chosen. The children all face the same direction and join hands with those on each side forming *streets* between the rows. Dropping hands, the children make a quarter turn and join hands again and form *alleys*. The chaser tries to tag the runner going up and down the streets or alleys but not breaking through or going under arms. The teacher aids the runner by calling "streets" or "alleys" at the proper time. At this command the children drop hands, turn, and grasp hands in the opposite direction, thus blocking the passage for the chaser. When caught, the runner and chaser select two others to take their places.

Application:

The children should be helped to note that the streets and alleys represent parallel lines, that no matter how far they are extended, they will not meet. When the teacher calls "alleys" and the children make a quarter turn, the children should note they have made a right angle turn and represent the concept of right angles.

Concept: Radius of a Circle
Activity: Jump The Shot

The children make a circle in groups of eight or ten, facing the center. One child stands in the center of the circle with a beanbag tied to the end of a rope. The center child swings the rope around in a large circle low to the ground in order for the beanbag to pass under the feet of those in the circle. The children in the circle attempt to jump over the beanbag as it passes beneath their feet. When the rope or beanbag touches a child, it is a point against him. The child with the lowest score wins at the end of a period one to two minutes long. The child in the center may then exchange places.

Application:

Children note that the radius of the circle is the length of the rope to which the beanbag is tied and is the distance from the center of the circle to the edge of the circle where the children stand. The teacher may draw a circle in order for the children to see this more clearly. The children can be helped to see the radius is the same from any part of the edge of the circle to the center.

Concept: Geometric Forms—Triangle

Activity: Triangle Run

A large triangle is marked off with a base at each corner. Three equal-sized teams are formed. One team stands behind each base. On a signal the first child of each team leaves his base and runs to his right around the triangle, touching each base on the way. When he returns to his base, the next child on his team does the same. The runners may pass each other, but they must touch each base as they run. The first team back in its original place wins.

Application:

This activity helps to show the shape of the triangle and demonstrates the concept of its perimeter. Children should note that the triangle must have three angles (where the bases are). At different times different-shape triangles may be marked off for the game to demonstrate the essence of the triangle is found in its three angles and three sides, not its shape.

Concept: Geometric Figures

Activity: Geometric Figure Relay

Two lines are drawn about thirty feet apart on a playing area. The class is divided into two teams. Both teams stand behind one of the lines. The teacher calls out the name of a geometric figure. The teams run across to the opposite line and form the figure. The team that forms the figure correctly first wins a point. The teams then line up behind that line, and when the teacher calls another figure, they run to the opposite line and again form the figure the teacher has called. The geometric figures will be those that the children have been working with, including the circle, square, rectangle, and triangle.

Application:

Children can gain the understanding of different geometric figures by acting out their shape in an individually involving and interesting activity.

Monetary System

Concept: Recognition of Coins—Penny, Nickel, Dime, Quarter
Activity: Stepping Stones

On the play area draw a stream with stepping stones arranged so that a child may take different paths across the stream. Each stepping stone will have a coin on it. The child is cautioned not to fall in the stream by making a mistake naming the coin. As the child chooses a stepping stone to cross the stream, he must name the coin and its value. Children at their seats watch for mistakes. A successful crossing scores one point for the child. The coins should be frequently changed.

Application:

This game provides the opportunity for children to recognize coins and their number value. Each child watching also is involved in the game while he keeps track of the child's answer who is crossing the stream.

Concept: Identification of Coins
Activity: Name The Coin

The class is divided into several teams. A box is given to each team containing a quantity of pennies, nickels, dimes, quarters, and half dollars. A leader from each team is assigned the task of keeping track of the team's money box. The teams stand in rows behind a line any specified distance from the leaders. The teacher calls out the name of any coin. The first member of each team runs to his team's money box, finds the coin in the box, shows it to the teacher, replaces it, and returns to the team. The child who first identifies a coin in the team box that the teacher called scores a point for his team. This continues, the teacher naming different coins for each member of the teams to find and identify. The team with the most points wins.

Application:

This game provides drill for quick recognition of coins following previous introduction of these coins and their value. A short review preceding the game helps children to recall the names and values of the coin.

Concept: Values of the Penney, Nickel, and Dime
Activity: Bank

One child is selected to be the Bank. The rest of the children stand at a starting line about twenty feet from the Bank. Bank calls out the number of pennies, nickels, or dimes a child may take. A penny is one small step; a nickel equals five penny steps; and a dime equals ten penny steps. Bank calls a child's name and says, "Harry, take three pennies." Harry must answer "May I?" Then Bank can say "Yes, you may" or "No, you may not." If Harry forgets to say "May I?" he must return to the starting line. The first child to reach the Bank becomes the Bank. All children should be called upon.

Application:

Children gain an understanding that a nickel equals five pennies and a dime equal ten pennies by taking the steps forward toward the Bank. The teacher might encourage each child to say before he moves forward how many steps he is allowed to take.

Concept: Value of Coins
Activity: Banker And The Coins

All the children of the class are given signs to wear denoting five cents, ten cents, quarters, fifty-cent pieces, nickels, and dimes. One child is the Banker. The Banker calls out different amounts of money up to one dollar. The children run and group themselves with other children until their group amounts to the value of the coin the Banker called. Every child who is part of a correct group gets a point.

Application:

The children become aware of the terms and values of different coins. They get practice in combining different amounts of money to arrive at a specific amount. To check that a group is correct, the teacher can help the whole class count it out. In this manner children can be helped to see how it takes two nickels to make one dime, and so on. They learn that five cents is the same as one nickel.

Chapter Seven

Teaching Slow Learners Science
Through Active Games

The opportunities for science experiences through active games are so numerous that it would perhaps be difficult to visualize an active game situation which is not related to science in some way. This is particularly true of physical science principles, since practically all voluntary body movements are based in some way upon one or more principles of physical science. For example, *equilibrium* is involved in many active game activities, and *motion* is the basis for almost all such activities.

The following is a summary of the active games along with the inherent science concepts, which are explained in detail in the ensuing section of the chapter. The games are grouped according to the major areas of the science curriculum. As previously stated, some games may have usefulness in developing concepts inasmuch as the concept is inherent in the activity itself. Other games are more appropriate for providing repetitive drill for skill development. The teacher might note many additional adaptations of games that can enrich the learnings of children in the science curriculum that are not mentioned specifically. It is hoped the teacher will find many other uses of the active games included in curriculum aspects not used in the activities presented.

CLASSIFICATION OF GAMES ACCORDING TO MAJOR AREAS IN ELEMENTARY SCHOOL SCIENCE

The following is a summary of the active games that contain science concepts and skills. Descriptions of the games follow the summary.

Concept	Game

The Universe and Earth:

Planets' Orbits Around the Sun	Planet Ball

Earth's Orbit Around the Sun	Earth's Orbit Relay Shadow Tag Night And Day

Eclipse of the Moon	Eclipse Tag

Force of Gravity	Catch The Cane Spoon Ball Carry Jump The Shot Basketball Twenty-One Planet Pull (Tide Pull)

Earth's Atmosphere	Hurricane Balloon Throw Pop The Balloon Relay Air Lift Water Cycle Relay

Earth's Surface	Zig-Zag Run

Conditions of Life:

Variety of Life	Squirrels In Trees Squirrels In Trees (Variation) Animal Relay Kangaroo Relay Snail Flowers And Wind

Interdependence of Life	Fox And Geese Spider And Flies Herds And Flocks Fox And Sheep Forest Lookout

Concept	*Game*
Chemical and Physical Changes:	
	Molecule Ball
	Molecule Pass
	Boiling Water
	Tag And Stoop
	Oxygen And Fuel
Light:	
	Light Bounce
	Heat And Light
	Spectrum Relay
Energy:	
Machines	Jump The Brook Relay
	Tug Of War
	Pin Guard
	Balloon Ball
	Siamese Twins
	Shoe Box Relay
	Hot Potato
	Net Ball
Electricity	Straddle Ball Roll
	Electric Ball
	Current Relay
	Lightning Relay
	Keep Away
Magnetism	Link Tag
	Hook-on Tag
	North And South
	Magnet, Magnet
Sound	Stoop Tag
Health:	
	Body Rebels
	Circle Pass

Concept	Game
	Beanbag Pass
	Body Relay
	Change Circle Relay

The Universe and Earth

Concept: Planets' Orbits Around the Sun

Activity: Planet Ball

The children form a single circle and count off by two's. The number one's step forward, turn, and face the number two's. The larger circle should be about four feet outside the inner circle. Two children, designated as team captains, stand opposite each other in the circle. The teacher stands in the center of the circle and represents the sun. Each captain has a ball which his team identifies as a planet. On a signal from the teacher each ball is passed counterclockwise to each team member until it travels all the way around the circle and back to the captain. Any child who is responsible for the ball striking the floor, either through a poor throw or a failure to catch the ball, has to recover the ball. As both circles pass the balls simultaneously, the time is kept and recorded. The group that passes the ball around their circle first wins or scores a point. Groups should exchange positions every several rounds.

Application:

Prior to playing the game, the children should note that the balls being passed around are the planets and that they are revolving around the sun, represented by the teacher. They should be helped to identify the balls that are being passed counterclockwise because that is the direction the planets orbit the sun. In using this game to illustrate the orbits of planets, it should be stressed that the path or orbit of the ball should be unbroken or uninterrupted. It should also be noted that each completed orbit was done with different amounts of time for each circle, that the inner circle tended to take less time to pass around the ball. Children can be encouraged to find out the differences in the orbits of the planets, as well as the varying lengths of times of these orbits.

Concept: Earth's Orbit Around the Sun
Activity: Earth's Orbit Relay

The children are arranged in two circles, each circle facing in. A captain is elected for each team, and they stand ready with balls in their hands. On a signal each captain starts his team's ball around by passing to the child on his right. Upon receiving the ball, each child spins around and passes the ball on to the next child on the right. As the ball makes a complete circuit back to the captain, he calls "One." The second time around he calls "Two." This procedure is repeated until the first team to pass the ball around the circle five times wins.

Application:

In this game the children need to be helped to see they are dramatizing the way the earth revolves around the sun. The entire circle becomes the complete orbit of the earth. The ball represents the earth, and as it is passed from one child to another, they can see how the earth revolves around the sun. Also, since each child must spin around with the ball before passing it on, the concept of earth's rotation on its axis may be shown. The children must always turn and pass counterclockwise, since that is the direction of the earth's orbit.

Concept: Length of Shadows According to Position of the Sun
Activity: Shadow Tag

The children are dispersed over the playing area, with one child designated as *it*. If *it* can step on the shadow of one of the children and call his name as he does, that child becomes *it*. A child may keep from being tagged by getting into the shade of a building or tree or by moving in such a way that *it* finds it difficult to step on his shadow.

Application:

In playing this game, the class can experiment by playing the game at different times of the day. The children can be helped to note the length of the shadow changes at different times of the day. They might measure and record these observations and seek to determine the reasons for the varying length of the shadows.

Concept: The Turning of the Earth on Its Axis Causes Day and Night

Activity: Night And Day

The children stand in a circle holding hands. One child in the center of the circle represents the Earth. As the children hold hands, they chant,

> Illery, dillery, daxis,
> The world turns on its axis.
> Isham, bisham bay,
> It turns from night to day.

While the children are chanting, Earth closes his eyes and turns slowly with one hand pointing towards the circle of children. As he rotates slowly with eyes closed (night), he continues to point with his hand. At the word *day* he stops and opens his eyes (day). Earth then runs after the child (to whom he is pointing at the word *day*) around the outside of the circle until he catches him. When the child is caught, he becomes the new Earth. The original Earth joins the circle, and the game continues. It might be advisable to use a blindfold that the child can slip off at the end of the verse.

Application:

The child in the center became the rotating Earth. When his eyes were closed, it became night, and when his eyes were open, it became day. The children might be encouraged to think of the child being pointed to as the sun, since it is day when the eyes are opened, and the sun causes day.

Concept: Eclipse of the Moon

Activity: Eclipse Tag

The children are group by couples facing each other. The couples are scattered in any way about the play area. One child is chosen for the runner and is called Earth. Another child is the chaser. On a signal the chaser tries to tag Earth. Earth is safe from being tagged when he runs and steps between two children who make up a couple. When Earth steps between the two children, he calls out "Eclipse." The chaser must then chase the child in the couple toward whom Earth turns his back. If the chaser is able to tag Earth, they exchange places.

Application:

This activity enables children to dramatize the concept of an eclipse of the moon so that they can see what occurs. The children should be helped to identify that when Earth steps between two children, the one he faces is the moon and his back is turned to the sun, and that the earth's shadow covers the moon.

Concept: Force of Gravity
Activity: Catch The Cane

The children are arranged in a circle, facing in. Each child is given a number. One child becomes *it* and stands in the center of the circle. He holds a stick or bat upright and balances it by putting his finger on the top of it. *It* calls one of the numbers assigned to the children in the circle. At the same time, he lets go of the stick. The child whose number is called dashes to get the stick before it falls to the ground. *It* dashes to the place occupied by the child whose number was called. If the child gets the stick in time, he returns to his place in the circle, and *it* holds the stick again. After the children have learned the game, several circles can be formed to provide active participation for more children. The teacher can provide for individual differences of poor performers by making the circle smaller.

Application:

The stick in this game represents the object which is being acted upon by the force of gravity. Every time *it* lets go of the stick, the stick begins to fall to the ground. This demonstrates the concept of the force of gravity to children. They may be helped to note that they must move faster than the force of gravity in order to catch the stick before it falls to the ground.

Concept: Force of Gravity
Activity: Spoon Ball Carry

The children are divided into several teams. The teams stand in rows behind a starting line. A large spoon holding a tennis ball is given to the first member of each team. On a given signal they run with the spoons and balls to a designated point and back. They then hand the spoons and balls to the next team members. The team finishing first wins. If a ball drops from a spoon, it must be scooped up with the spoon and not touched otherwise.

Some variety can be created by using balls of different sizes and weights. These varying balls can be used at set intervals during one relay or in separate relay races.

Application:

The concept of gravity is an inherent part of this activity. The children's attention should be directed as to why the ball seldom drops from the spoon and why, when it does, it falls down, not up. The use of a variety of sizes and weights of balls may create curiosity on the part of the children. Children can be helped to note that they have more success in carrying a larger and heavier ball than one which is smaller and lighter. This experience can be directed toward further research by the children on questions posed by the group.

Concept: Force of Gravity

Activity: Jump The Shot

The children form a circle, with one child in the center. The center child has a length of rope with a beanbag attached to one end. He holds the rope at the other end and swings the rope around close to the ground. The children in the circle must jump over the rope to keep from being hit. Any child who fails to jump and is hit receives a point against him. The child with the least number of points at the end of the game is the winner.

Application:

The game is played in small groups, and each child should have a turn to be in the center and swing the rope. The teacher might ask the children what they felt on the other end of the rope as they swung it around, that is, if they felt a pull. The teacher can ask what would happen if the rope broke or they let go of their end. This can be demonstrated. Further questions can lead to what kept the rope and beanbag from flying off during the game, that an inward pull on the rope kept the beanbag moving in a circular pattern. The teacher might also relate this to the manner planets travel in a circular orbit around the sun and the moon circles the earth because of gravitational force.

Concept: Force of Gravity

Activity: Basketball Twenty-One

The children form teams. The teams make rows behind the

free-throw line. The first child takes a shot and scores two points if he makes it. He then recovers the ball and shoots again from closer to the basket. If he makes this shot, he scores one point. The teams take turns at the basket, shooting the long and short shots. The first team reaching twenty-one points wins.

Application:

This game can be used during the study of gravitational force. The teacher can demonstrate that the ball must be aimed higher when shooting farther away from the basket to overcome the force of gravity, which pulls the ball toward the earth as it travels through the air. The children can note that if the ball is thrown directly toward the basket without aiming higher to compensate for gravitational pull, the ball will go under the basket. Children can experiment with different types of throws from different distances from the basket.

Concept: Gravitational Pull—Of Tides, Planets
Activity: Planet Pull (Tide Pull)

The children are divided into two teams. One can be named Earth and the other Moon. The first child on each team kneels down on all fours, facing a member of the other team. There is a line drawn on the floor between them. Each child has a collar made from a towel or piece of strong cloth placed around his neck. Each child grabs both ends of the other person's towel. The object is for each one to try to pull the other one across the line. The child who succeeds scores a point for his team. Each child on the team does the same. The team with the most points wins.

Application:

This game can be used to demonstrate the gravitational pull of earth and the moon, or the planets and the sun. It might be pointed out that a larger child often was stronger and was usually able to pull a smaller child across the line, just as with members of the solar system being pulled to the largest member, the sun.

Concept: Earth's Atmosphere—Wind Is Moving Air
Activity: Hurricane

The children are divided into two teams. Each team lines up on either side of a small playing area with lines drawn six feet apart on each side. In the center is a small, light object such as a ping-pong ball. Each child has a fan made of newspaper, cardboard, or some other type of suitable material. On a given signal the children fan the ball toward the opposite goal line. Each time the ball goes over the goal, a point is scored. The team having five points wins the game.

Application:

In this activity children can see that their fans create a wind. The wind is moving and makes the ball move. Children might experiment with different types of fans and ways of fanning to see if they can create stronger air movements.

Concept: Earth's Atmosphere—Air Has Pressure and Pushes
Against Things

Activity: Balloon Throw

Children take turns throwing an inflated toy balloon. A line is marked on the floor, and the thrower may use any method of throwing as long as he does not step on or over this line. His throw is measured from the line to the spot his balloon first touches the floor. The child with the longest throw wins.

Application:

The children can experience the feeling of throwing an object so light in relation to size that the resistance of air prevents the object from traveling in an arc as expected. In substituting a playground ball, the children can note the difference in the distance it travels with the same type of throw. A tennis ball can also be used for comparison of distance traveled and action of throwing.

Concept: Earth's Atmosphere—Air Takes Up Space and Pushes
Against Things

Activity: Pop The Balloon Relay

The children are divided into relay teams of equal numbers. On the floor beside each child is placed a small balloon that has not been blown up. On a signal the first child on each team runs to the front of the room with his balloon, blows up and pops it, then returns to his place. When his balloon pops, the next child picks up his, waits for the first child to return to his place, and then continues in the same manner. The first team to finish with all the team members popping their balloons and returning to their places wins. Since this may be a noisy type relay, it might be advisable to have it outside rather than in the classroom.

Application:

As each child blows air into the balloon, he is able to see that the sides of the balloon are pushed out by the air that has filled up the space inside. Likewise, as he pops the balloon, he can see that the air is released and the sides of the balloon are no longer pushed out.

Concept: Earth's Atmosphere—Force or Lift of Air

Activity: Air Lift

The children are divided into teams of four to six members each. One team stands on one side of a net stretched across the center of the court. (The size of the court may vary.) The game is started by one child throwing a rubber ring over the net. Any opposing team member may catch the ring and throw it back. The ring may not be relayed to another child on the same team. Play continues until a point is scored. A point is scored each time the ring hits the ground in the opponents' court or when any of the following fouls are committed:

1. Hitting the net with the ring.

2. Throwing the ring under the net.

3. Relaying the ring or having two teammates touch it in succession.

4. Throwing the ring out of bounds if opposing team does not touch it.

The team scored upon puts the ring in play again. Five to fifteen points is a game, depending on the skill of the group.

Application:

The ring is used to represent an airplane, and the children's attempts to toss it over the net without allowing it to fall can be compared to *lift*. In attempting to toss the ring over the net, many fouls may be committed, and it should be pointed out that this is due to both the insufficient amount of force of air, the downward pull of gravity, and also poor aiming. In most cases more force or lift is needed to launch a ring, or plane. When each point is made, it can be referred to as a plane successfully launched. The children might be encouraged to find out how planes are launched from aircraft carriers. They may conclude that a plane must have an enormous lift before it can rise. It can be further pointed out that the force that produces the lift to cause a plane to rise is caused by movements of air and that this movement produces low pressures over the top of the wings and high pressures under the bottom of the wings.

Concept: Earth's Atmosphere—Water Cycle
Activity: Water Cycle Relay
The children are divided into teams of six children each. Each child is assigned a part of the water cycle in the order of the process, for example, (a) water vapor, (b) rain, (c) land, (d) stream, (e) river, and (f) ocean. The teams are seated in rows or stand in rows close enough to be able to pass a ball from one child to the next. On a signal the first child of each team calls his part of the water cycle (water vapor), passes the ball to the second child on his team, and runs to the end of his team's line. The second child calls out his part (rain), passes the ball to the next team member, and moves back in the same manner. This procedure continues until each team has made three complete cycles. The first team to finish wins.

Application:
The cycle is represented by the children moving in turn. As the children pass the ball, it should be emphasized that the various stages are represented by each child. It is important that the children note the correct order within the cycle and situate themselves in the line accordingly. The ball represents water regardless of the form it takes within the cycle. The game may be adapted by changing the rain part of the cycle to snow or sleet and by adding brooks and bays if the children so choose.

Concept: Earth's Surface—Coastlines and Mountains Cause
              Ocean Currents and Winds to Change Direction
Activity: Zig-Zag Run
The class is divided into teams. The teams form rows behind a starting line. Four ten pins or other objects are placed in a

line four feet apart in front of each team. On a signal the first child on each team runs to the right of the first pin and to the left of the second pin and so on in a zig-zag fashion, going around the last pin. He returns to place in the same manner. The second child proceeds as the first child. If a child knocks down a pin, he must set it up before he continues. The team finishing first wins.

Application:

The children on the teams can represent the ocean currents and winds. The pins can represent the coastlines and mountains. It might be helpful to use children for the objects, and they could change their position slightly each time. The children must go around the objects in order to reach their goal. If the objects were not there, the children could travel in a straight line to the goal and back. By having to go around the objects children show how the ocean currents and winds have to change direction when they meet obstacles.

Conditions of Life

Concept: Variety of Life—Animals Live in Many Kinds of Homes

Activity: Squirrels In Trees

With the exception of one child the children are arranged in groups of three around the play area. Two of the children in each group face each other and hold hands, forming a *hollow tree*. The third child is a Squirrel and stands between the other two children. The extra child, who is also a Squirrel, stands near the center of the play area. If there is another extra child, there can be two Squirrels. The teacher calls "Squirrel in the tree, listen to me. Find yourself another tree." On the word *tree,* all Squirrels must run and get into a different hollow tree, and the extra Squirrel also tries to find a tree. There is always one extra Squirrel who does not have a tree. At different points in the game, the teacher should have the children change places. The game can then be adapted for other animals such as beavers in dams, foxes or rabbits in holes, bears in caves, and the like.

Application:

In playing this game, children can name other animals and the kinds of homes in which they live. They can be encouraged to figure out how they could dramatize the different types of homes animals have, as the two children form the hollow tree.

Concept: Variety of Life—Some Animals Hibernate in Winter
Activity: Squirrels In Trees (Variation)

The regular game of Squirrels in Trees is played. One child is the extra Squirrel. The other children stand in groups of three about the play area. In the groups, two of the childfren face each other and hold hands while the third child, the Squirrel, stands between them. The leader calls out "Squirrels in the tree, listen to me. It is sunny and warm; find yourself something to eat." On the word *eat,* all the Squirrels must leave their tree and hunt for food. When the leader calls "Hibernate," all the Squirrels, including the extra Squirrel, must try to find a hollow tree. There will always be one extra Squirrel. The children should be encouraged to be brave while looking for food and not stay too close to a hollow tree.

Application:

This variation of the game emphasizes the hibernation concept. By the children dramatizing the concept of food gathering and hibernation, they are helped to see the winter life patterns of some animals.

Concept: Variety of Life—Animals Move About in Different
Ways
Activity: Animal Relay

The children divide into several teams. The teams stand in rows behind a line about twenty feet from a goal line. The object of the relay is for each team member to move forward to the goal line and return to his place at the rear of his team, moving as quickly as he can according to the type of animal movement assigned. Relays may be varied by the children going to the goal line and back doing the following imitations of various animals:

Donkey Walk—traveling on all fours, imitating a donkey's kick and bray.

Crab Walk—walking on all fours, face up.

Bear Walk—walking on all fours, feet going outside of hands.

Rabbit Hop—child moves forward, bringing his feet forward between his hands.

Elephant Walk—child bends forward, hands flat on floor with knees straight and then backwards keeping knees and elbows straight all the time.

On a signal the teams proceed with the relay, using the movement indicated by the teacher. The first team finished wins.

Application:

By dramatizing the various movements of animals, children are helped to learn about the differences among animals. Children can be encouraged to figure out ways of moving to represent many types of animals.

Concept: Variety of Life—Animals Move About in Different Ways

Activity: Kangaroo Relay

The children are divided into several teams. The teams in rows line up behind a starting line. About thirty feet away or less, parallel to the starting line, is a goal line. The first child of each team places the ball between his knees and without touching the ball, jumps to the goal line. He then takes the ball in his hands, runs back to the starting line, and gives the ball to the next child, who must be behind the starting line. The team members proceed in the same manner. The first team finished wins.

Application:

Despite their awkward size, kangaroos have an effective means of moving over the ground to escape their enemies. By executing the kangaroo movement stunt in this game, the children are better able to understand the method of mobility of this animal. The teacher might have the children contrast this method with the way other animals move by acting out different animal movements.

Concept: Variety of Life—Animals Escape Their Enemies in Many Ways

Activity: Snail

The children stand in a row with the teacher as the leader at the end of the line. While singing the first verse, the leader walks around in a circle and continues to walk so that the circle becomes smaller. During the singing of the second verse the leader reverses his direction to enlarge the circle.

Hand in hand we circle now,
Like a snail into his shell
Coming nearer, coming nearer,
In we go and in we go.
Aren't you glad this little shell
Keeps us all and holds us well?

Hand in hand we circle now,
Like a snail just from its shell
Going further, going further,
Out we go and out we go.
Aren't you glad this little shell
Kept us all and held us well?

Application:

The concept of animals needing protection from their enemies and employing various means for protection is inherent in this activity. Children might be encouraged to find out other ways animals seek protection from their natural enemies.

Concept: Variety of Life—Wind is Moving Air and Transports
  Some Kinds of Seeds
Activity: Flowers And Wind

The children are divided into two teams, each team having a home marked off at opposite ends of the play area with a neutral space between. One team represents a flower (deciding among themselves which flower they shall represent, as daises, lilies, and so on). They then walk over near the home line of the opposite team. The opposing team (representing the wind) stands in a line within their home area, ready to run. They guess what the flower chosen by their opponents may be. As soon as the right flower is named, the entire team must turn and run home, the wind chasing them. Any children caught by the wind before reaching home must join the wind team. The remaining flowers repeat their play, taking a different flower name each time. This continues until all of the flowers have been caught. The teams then exchange, and the flower team becomes the wind team.

Application:

In this game some of the children represent the wind, and

the others represent the flowers and/or seeds. As the flowers walk to the wind home, they represent the flower growing through the summer. When the wind guesses the name of the flower, this represents the end of the growth period. As the flowers begin to run, they represent the seeds, and the children chasing them represent the wind carrying the seeds along. The flowers running also represent the seeds dispersing in different directions being borne by the wind.

Concept: Interdependence of Life
Activity: Fox And Geese

Two lines are drawn on opposite ends of the play area. One child is the Fox and stands in the center of the play area. The other children are the Geese and stand behind one of the end lines. When the Geese are ready, the Fox calls "Run!" and the Geese must then run and attempt to cross the opposite end line before the Fox can catch them. The Geese are not safe until they have crossed this line. The children who are tagged by the Fox must help the Fox tag the remaining geese the next time. The Geese who have not been tagged line up at the end line and on a signal from the Fox, run back to the original starting line. When the Geese have run three times, a new Fox is chosen.

Application:

Through this game the children learn that animals eat other animals as a means of survival and that these types of animals are called carnivorous. The children might find out various animals that are natural enemies and substitute their names for fox and geese.

Concept: Interdependence of Life
Activity: Spider And Flies

Two goal lines are drawn at opposite ends of the play area and a circle equal distance between two goal lines. The children stand around the edge of the circle, facing the center. One child, the Spider, sits in the center of the circle. The other children are Flies. The Spider sits very still while the other children, the Flies, walk or skip around the circle, clapping their hands as they go. At any time the Spider may suddenly jump up and chase the Flies. When he does, the Flies run toward either goal. A Fly tagged before reaching one of the goal lines becomes a Spider and joins the first Spider in the circle. The original Spider always gives the starting signal to chase the Flies, and other Spiders may not leave the circle to chase the Flies until he gives this signal. The last child caught becomes the next Spider.

Application:

The children should be encouraged to cultivate their quickness. The Spider should be urged to leap up suddenly in order to surprise the Flies. In this game the children can be helped to understand the interdependence of animals for food by the dramatizing of animals hunting each other for food and the victims seeking shelter for protection.

Concept: Interdependence of Life—Some Animals Live in Social
              Groups in Which They Work Together to Survive

Activity: Herds And Flocks

A starting line is drawn. The children are divided into several teams and stand one behind the other in relay formation at the starting line. A goal line is drawn thirty to forty feet in front of the starting line. Each member of the relay team is to perform a different action while going to and from the goal line. The teacher assigns the movement to each team member, for example, the first child on each team is to perform one task, the second child on each team to perform another. Some of the suggested actions are the following:

Walk with stiff knees.
Place hands on hips, hold feet together, and hop.
Proceed in squat position to goal, run to starting line.
Hop on one foot.
Skip to goal, sit on floor, and skip to starting line.
Swing arms in circular motion while walking quickly.
Place hands on head and run.

The signal is given for the first child from each team to proceed with his assigned action. As soon as he returns to the starting line, he touches the extended right hand of the second child on his team and then goes to the end of the line. The second child goes forth performing his designated action. Play continues until one team has had all of its members complete their performances and return to their places. This team is the winner.

Application:

The children can learn in playing this game that to win, all the children must cooperate and perform their different actions in an acceptable manner and as quickly as they can. This can be compared with certain animal groups whose different members perform various tasks for the safety and well-being of the group. The concept can be further integrated into the game by helping children to note that just as some of the actions in the game are difficult to do, so are some of the things that have to be done in order to survive. The children might be encouraged to find out the various roles different members of animal groups perform in order to protect the members of the group from their enemies and to obtain food. They can be helped to identify which type of group member is assigned the different roles, for example, the strong to hunt for food and the older for *lookouts*.

Concept: Interdependence of Life—Animals Have To Protect Themselves From One Another

Activity: Fox and Sheep

One child is selected to be the Fox who stands in his den, a place marked off on one side of a play area. The rest of the children are the Sheep. They stand in the Sheepfold, another area marked on the opposite side of the play area. The remaining part of the play area is called the Meadow. The Fox leaves his den and wanders around the Meadow, whereupon the Sheep sally forth and approaching the Fox, ask him, "Are you hungry, Mr. Fox?" Should the Fox say "No, I'm not," the Sheep are safe. When the Fox says "Yes, I am!" the Sheep must run for the sheepfold, as the Fox may then begin to chase them. The Fox tags as many Sheep as he can before they find shelter in the fold. Those Sheep who are caught must go to the Fox's den and thereafter assist the Fox in capturing Sheep. The original Fox is always the first one to leave the den. He also is the Fox who answers the Sheep's questions. The last Sheep caught becomes the Fox for the next game. This game can be adapted by using other animals who are natural enemies to each other as cat and mouse, hound and rabbit, or fox and geese.

Application:

In this activity the children dramatize the interdependence of animals, that some animals need others for food and are natural enemies. The children can sense the fear of the chase and the need to protect oneself. The children may find out what are the names of the different types of shelter of the different animals.

Concept: Interdependence of Life—Conservation of Forests
Activity: Forest Lookout

The children form a circle and count off by two's. All the one's form a circle; all the two's form a second circle so that there is a double circle with all the children facing inward. The children on the inside circle represent trees. Each member of the outside circle represents a Fire Fighter and stands behind one of the trees. One child is the Lookout; he stands in the center of the group. The Lookout calls loudly, "Fire in the forest! Run, run, run!" while clapping his hands. All the Fire Fighters in the outside circle begin running to the left. While the Fire Fighters are running, the Lookout quietly takes a place in front of one of the trees. The runners who observe the Lookout doing this, do likewise. The Fire Fighter left without a tree becomes the Lookout for the next game, and the trees become the Fire Fighters for the next game.

Application:

This game helps to emphasize the importance of protecting the forests from fire. It can be brought out that many animals lose their homes if the trees burn and that small plants are also destroyed.

Chemical and Physical Changes

Concept: Movement of Molecules in Solids, Liquids, and Gases
Activity: Molecule Ball

The children arrange themselves in a circle. The group then counts off by two's. The number one's face inward, and the number two's face outward, that is, one's and two's are facing each other. Each captain has a ball that is to be moved around the circle until it travels back to the captain. The exact manner in which the balls are to be moved around the circles is determined by the leader calling "solid," "liquid," or "gas." When "gas" is called, the ball is to be thrown from one child to the next; when "liquid" is called, the ball is to be bounced from one child to the next; and when "solid" is called, the ball is to be passed to the next child. When the ball completes the circle, that team which does so first is declared the winner. Whenever a child drops or does not catch the ball passed to him, he must retrieve the ball, return to his place in the circle, and then continue to move the ball to the next child.

Application:

The use of *solid, liquid,* and *gas* as call words to change the speed of the balls' progress around the circles emphasizes the difference in speed of molecule's movement in solids, liquids, and gases. The children can be helped to note that the method of moving the ball around the circle relates to the speed of the movement of molecules in these different states of matter.

Concept: Molecules Are in Rapid and Ceaseless Motion
Activity: Molecule Pass

The class is divided into four groups, with each group standing in a straight line. The four groups form a rectangle with each group representing one side of the rectangle. The captain of each group stands near the center of the rectangle in front of his group. On a signal each captain throws his ball to his group, starting at the right. As each child receives the ball, he throws it back to his captain and assumes a squatting position. When the captain throws the ball to the last child in his group, he runs to the right of his group as the rest of the children stand. The last child on the left runs with the ball to the captain's place, and the procedure is repeated.

Application:

Each ball represents a molecule of matter. The balls are kept in motion at all times. The children can be helped to note that the ball (the molecule of matter) has to be kept moving. This can lead to a discussion of molecules of different substances: the greater space and rapid movement of molecules of gases (depending on area temperature), the less space and less rapid movement of molecules of liquids, and the lesser space and least rapid movement of molecules of solids.

Concept: Elements in a Compound (the Composition of Molecules) Cannot Be Separated by Physical Means

Activity: Boiling Water

Two or more circles are formed. Each circle is given one or more balls. A kitchen cooking pot is set along the sidelines of the play area. One child in each circle is the leader. When the teacher calls "cold water," the children in each circle pass the ball from one child to the next. Whenever the teacher calls "warm water," the children roll the ball across the center of the circle from one to another. If the teacher calls "boiling water," the children throw the ball to different ones in the circle. When the teacher calls "water vapor," the ball is immediately thrown to the circle leader, who then runs with it to the kitchen pot on the sidelines. The team whose leader reaches the pot first wins.

Application:

The ball represents a molecule of water. The ball is one of the surface molecules. At first, the molecule moves slowly (cold water). When the water begin to warm up, the speed of the molecule increases (warm water). As the water approaches boiling point, the speed of molecules increases (boiling water) until it acquires sufficient motion to escape to the air (water vapor). The ball (molecule) has not been altered. It has moved from one place (the liquid state or water) to another place (gaseous state or water vapor).

Concept: Chain Reaction Comes From One Molecule Hitting Another (or Neutrons in Radioactive Materials)

Activity: Tag And Stoop

The children are scattered over the playing area. One child is *it* and tries to tag two children, one with each hand. When *it* tags the first child, he then grasps the hand of that child. The two continue running after other children until *it* is able to tag a second child. *It* then stands still and gets down in a stooping position. The two children tagged now each try to tag two others and then they stoop down. The four children tagged now continue in the same manner. The object of the game is to see how long it takes for everyone to be tagged.

Application:

In trying to demonstrate chain reaction, the increasingly powerful effect of a small beginning should be brought out. As the children watch the spread of those who are being tagged, they can see this effect.

Concept: Burning Is Oxidation: The Chemical Union of a Fuel With Oxygen

Activity: Oxygen And Fuel

One child is chosen to be Fuel and another child is Oxygen. The remaining children join hands and form a circle, with Fuel in the center of the circle and Oxygen on the outside of the circle. The children in the circle try to keep Oxygen from getting into the circle and catching Fuel. If Oxygen gets in the circle, the children in the circle then let Fuel out of the circle and try to keep Oxygen in, but they must keep their hands joined at all times. When Oxygen catches Fuel, the game is over, and they join the circle while two other children become Fuel and Oxygen. If Fuel is not caught in a specified period of time, a new Oxygen can be selected.

Application:

One child represents the fuel (as trees in a forest) and another the oxygen (the air). The children in the circle are the preventers of fire. If Oxygen catches Fuel and ignites him by tagging him, a fire is started. Then the game is over. In this manner children can be helped to note that oxygen feeds fires and that oxygen must be kept from fires that have been started in order to put them out. The children might be encouraged to find out ways that fires are smothered, depending upon the type of burning material.

Light

Concept: When Light Strikes a Solid Object, It Bounces

Activity: Light Bounce

The children are divided into several teams. Two lines are marked on the floor or play area, parallel to a blank wall. One line is drawn six inches from the wall and is the goal line. The second line is drawn twelve feet from the wall. Behind this second line, the teams stand in rows. Each team is given a small wooden block. The first child on each team takes turns throwing his block. If the block lands between the goal line and the wall, a point is scored for that team. If the block falls outside the goal line, each other team gets one point. Each child on the teams proceeds in the same manner until each child has had a throw. The team with the highest score wins.

Application:

Children can be helped to note that the wooden blocks rebound from the wall just as light rays do upon coming in contact with a solid object.

Concept: Heat and Light Can Be Reflected
Activity: Heat And Light

The children are divided into several teams. The teams make rows at a specified distance from the blank wall of a building. The first child on each team throws a ball against the building and catches it as it bounces back to him, passes it over his head to the next child on the team, and then moves to the end of the line. The team to complete the procedure first wins.

Application:

Attention can be called to the fact that just as the ball hits the wall and bounces back, so light and heat are reflected, for example, light and heat are reflected (or bounced off) by a mirror or other shiny surface.

Concept: A Prism Can Separate a Beam of White Light Into a
Spectrum
Activity: Spectrum Relay

The class is divided into two teams so that there will be seven children on each team. Each team forms a row behind a starting line. Then the children on each team are assigned a specific color of the spectrum and stand in the correct order that colors appear in the spectrum, for example, red, orange, yellow, green, blue, indigo, and violet. Each child is given the appropriate color tag to pin on his clothing so that his teammates can quickly see where

to line up. Those children who are not assigned to a relay team
are the Prism and stand at a given distance away from the starting
line and space themselves several feet apart, facing the relay teams.
On a signal all the children on each team must run between and
around back of the children standing a distance away (the prism)
and return to the starting line. The team members must then
join hands so that each team finishes by being lined up in the
correct order of colors in the spectrum behind the starting line.
The first team lined up correctly behind the starting line wins.
A few children may change places with those who did not have
a chance to run in the first relay.

Application:

This relay provides children with the opportunity to dramatize
the concept of the prism. The teams represent the beams of light
before passing through the glass prism (represented by the children standing a distance away) and that after they passed through
the glass prism, they then represented the band of colors called
the *visible spectrum*. During the discussion it can be pointed out
that each color of light travels through the glass prism at a different speed. The children can be encouraged to find about different
things in nature that serve as prisms to create visible spectrums.

Energy

Concept: Energy Is Needed To Stop Rapidly Moving Objects
(Newton's Law of Inertia)

Activity: Jump The Brook Relay

The children are divided into teams. The teams stand in rows
behind the starting line. The goal line is a good running distance
away. Two lines, approximately three feet apart, are drawn
parallel about ten feet from the goal line. The space between the
two center lines represents the brook. On a signal the captain of
each team runs to the brook, stops, jumps over the brook with two
feet together, runs to the finish line, and then returns to the starting line in the same way. He touches the second child on his team
and then goes to the rear of his team. This procedure is continued
until all the team members have jumped the brook. The team
finishing first wins. Any child who fails to jump the brook (and

so falls in) must return to the starting line and begin his turn again. The teacher may therefore adjust the size of the brook according to the limitations of the group.

Application:

Children can discover that it takes great effort on their part to stop themselves when they reached the brook in order to make their jump with two feet together. When they stop suddenly, they find that while they might be able to stop their feet, the upper part of their bodies continues to move forward. Actually trying to stop on their part involves body energy or force. The children can also be encouraged to experiment and find that the faster they run, the more energy they have to expend to stop themselves.

Concept: Principle of Inertia

Activity: Tug Of War

The class is divided into two teams. A line is drawn between the teams as a goal line. The teams line up on each side of the goal line. Each member grabs hold of the rope in a single file fashion at the same distance from the goal line. Both teams are now in position to pull against each other. On a signal they begin pulling. The team that pulls the other over the goal the first wins the game.

Application:

If each team in the Tug of War pulls just as hard as the other, there is no motion in either direction. If one team is stronger than the other, then there will be an unbalanced force, causing the other team to be pulled over the goal line in the direction of the stronger team.

Concept: A Body Left to Itself, Free From the Action of Other Bodies, Will, if at Rest, Remain at Rest

Activity: Pin Guard

The children form a circle. Ten pins or other suitable objects are set up in the middle of the circle. One child is selected as a Guard to protect the pins. On a signal the children start rolling a ball to knock over the pins. The Guard tries to keep the ball away from the pins by kicking it back toward the circle. The child who succeeds in knocking down a pin becomes the new Guard.

Application:

The pins in this game represent the body at rest (inertia) and the ball the force that puts the body in motion. It can be pointed out to the children that the pins in the center of the circle remain at rest until an outside force (the ball) strikes the pins and puts them in motion.

Concept: Laws of Motion (Acceleration Is in Proportion to the Force That Caused It and in the Same Direction as That force)

Activity: Balloon Ball

The class is divided into two teams. Each team divides into three groups. If a classroom is used, rows one, three, and five are team A. Rows two, four, and six are team B. The space on the outside of the first and sixth row are the goals. If the game is played outside, the teams may sit in the same manner with lines drawn outside the first and sixth row to serve as goal lines. A balloon is tossed into the air in the center of the room by the teacher. The seated children strike the balloon with the open hand and try to get it over their opponent's goal. The children may not strike the balloon with their fists or leave their seats. If either of these violations is committed, the balloon is tossed into the air by a member of the team that committed the violation. Each goal counts one point. The team scoring the greater number of points wins the game. If too many goals are made, one child from each team may be chosen to be goalkeeper. They may stand and try to prevent the balloon from striking the floor in their respective goal areas.

Application:

It can be pointed out to the children that when they hit the balloon, the balloon moves in the same direction as their hand. They also can be helped to notice that if the balloon is tapped lightly, it moves a short distance, and if it is hit hard, the balloon moves a long distance. This game dramatizes the concepts involved in Newton's laws of motion in a way children can see and understand.

Concept: Friction
Activity: Siamese Twins

The children get in pairs and sit back to back with arms folded and legs extended straight ahead and together. The object is to see which pair can stand first with feet together while maintaining the folded arm position.

Application:

Before the game children can talk about some of the results of friction, such as heat and the resulting problems confronting scientists who design space missiles. The class might discuss ways in which friction helps us, for example, the friction between feet and ground when we walk and how we use snow tires or chains to provide friction in snow and icy weather. During and after this game the teacher can help the children see how the friction of their feet against the floor keeps them from sliding down. After the game the children might plan to chart lists of ways in which friction helps us.

Concept: Friction
Activity: Shoe Box Relay

The class is divided into several teams. The teams stand in rows behind a starting line twenty to thirty feet away from a goal line. Each team is given two large shoe boxes. The first child places his feet in the shoe boxes and advances to the goal line by sliding his feet along in a walking motion. When he crosses the goal line, he then returns to the starting line. The second child then places his feet in the shoe boxes and proceeds in the same manner. The first team who completes the race with all the team members in line behind the starting line wins. It is a good idea to have extra shoe boxes in case one becomes mutilated.

Application:

From this activity the children can be shown that friction occurs whenever two surfaces rub together, and the larger the two areas moving against each other, the greater the friction. The children might discuss how tired their legs get and how much more difficult this means of locomotion is than walking.

Concept: Machines Make Work Easier—Arm as Lever

Activity: Hot Potato

The class is divided into even number lines of five to six children each, separated at arms length from each other. Each line faces another line five to twenty feet away. Each child has a turn holding a ball at chest height in one hand and hitting it with the palm of the other hand, directing the ball to the line facing him. Each child of the opposite line scores one point for each ball he catches. The child who catches the ball then proceeds to hit the ball back to the opposite line, who tries to catch the ball to score a point. The child with the highest score wins.

Application:

The use of the arm as a lever can be demonstrated in this activity. The teacher might draw a picture on the blackboard to show children how the arm works as a lever.

Concept: The Lever (In the Third-Class Lever the Effort Is Placed Between the Load and the Fulcrum)

Concept: The Greater a Force Applied to a Mass, the Greater the Acceleration of That Mass Will Be

Activity: Net Ball (Note: Two concepts can be developed by Net Ball.)

Before this activity the children can be told that serving is a basic skill used in the game of net ball and that for a successful game of net ball, it is necessary to learn to serve the ball properly. The server stands on the end line facing the net. He holds the ball in his left hand about waist height in front of him and to the right. He hits the ball underhand with his right hand (heel of the hand or fist). The weight of his body is transferred forward to the left foot as the right arm moves forward in a follow-through movement.

The children are divided into two groups, each group spaced in a pattern on one side of the net facing the other group. After the teacher demonstrates several times, each child is given the opportunity to attempt to serve the ball two or three times. Following practice, the game is started by one child serving the ball over the net. Any opposing team member may hit the ball with his hands (heel of the hand or fist) back to the other side of the net. The ball may not be relayed to another child on the same team. Play continues until a point is scored. A point is scored each time the ball hits the ground in the opponents' court or any of the following fouls are committed:

1. Hitting the net with the ball.
2. Hitting the ball under the net.
3. Relaying the ball or having two teammates touch it in succession.
4. Hitting the ball out of bounds if opposing team does not touch it.

Application: (The Lever)

During the practice it can be shown how the arm has acted as a lever in the serving action, that the elbow joint was the fulcrum, the forearm was the effort, and the ball was the load. Children can then be encouraged to find other examples that would illustrate this type of lever, for example, a man swinging a golf club or a boy swinging at a ball with a bat.

Application: (Force and Acceleration)

It can be noted that the servers have difficulty getting the ball in the opposite court, that the ball either fails to go over the net or it is hit out of bounds on the opposite side. The teacher can stop the activity to ask what makes the ball go out of bounds. The children might note that it was hit too hard. If the ball fails to go over the net, it can be pointed out it was not hit hard enough. The teacher can then ask the class to explain what factor influences the speed and distance the ball travels (the force of the serve or how hard the ball is hit that governs the acceleration of the ball). The children can be encouraged to apply this concept to other types of activities such as batting a baseball, peddling a bike, or a rocket booster.

Concept: Electrical Current Must Travel in a Circuit

Activity: Straddle Ball Roll

The children line up one behind the other in teams of eight to ten. All stand with their feet apart. The leader of each team holds a basketball or a similar-sized rubber playground ball. On a signal the leader stoops and rolls the ball back between the legs of all the members of his team. When the last player on the team secures the ball, he holds it up. The team getting the ball up first wins one point. The last child of each team now moves up to be the leader. On a signal he rolls the ball and again the last child on the team holds it up as soon as he gets it. A scorer at the blackboard or out-of-doors keeps track of the points made for each team. The team making the most points after all have had a turn to roll the ball wins the game.

Application:

The ball is the current of electricity. The first member of each team is the source, and the circuit is the path between the children's feet and legs. The first child might be considered the switch to turn on the current. The circuit may be broken if the ball goes outside a child's legs. (A point might be scored against the team if this occurs.) The electrical current continues (the ball being put back into play) when the circuit is repaired.

Concept: Electricity Is the Flow of Electrons in a Closed Circuit
Activity: Electric Ball

The children form a circle and join hands (representing a closed circuit). The children are to move a soccer ball or similar type ball if a soccer ball is not available around the inside of the circle. The ball represents the current or flow of electrons. The children move the ball from one child to the next by using the instep of the foot as in Soccer. The object of the game is to keep the ball moving around the circle and preventing the ball from leaving the circle by blocking it with the feet or legs while keeping the hands joined at all times. If the ball leaves the circle (an open or broken circuit), the two children between whom the ball escapes the circle are each given a point. The game continues with the children having the lowest scores as winners.

Application:

Children are able to see this concept demonstrated in this game, that of the flow of electrons through a closed circuit by passing the ball around the circle and that a broken circuit prevents the flow of electricity when the ball leaves the circle.

Concept: Electricity Is the Flow of Electrons in a Closed Circuit
Activity: Current Relay

Children are arranged in teams in rows. Each child reaches back between his legs with his right hand and grasps the left hand of the child immediately in back of him. On a signal the teams thus joined together race to the goal line some thirty to forty feet from the starting line and then race back to the starting line. The team finishing first with the line unbroken wins.

Application:

The joined hands of the members of the teams represent the closed circuit. As long as the circuit remains unbroken, electricity can flow (the children could move their feet and proceed with the race). If the circuit is broken, it has to be repaired (the children rejoin hands) before electricity can continue to flow and the team can move forward again.

Concept: Lightning Is Electricity
Activity: Lightning Relay

The class is divided into several teams. The first child in each team toes a starting line. On a signal he jumps. Someone marks the heel print of each jumper. The next child on each team steps forward to the heel mark of the first child, toes this mark, and jumps. This procedure is continued until every child on each team has jumped. The team having jumped the greatest distance wins.

Application:

Each child is electricity or lightning *jumping* from one cloud to another. The concept of lightning being electricity gathering in a cloud and jumping to the ground or to another cloud can be noted by the children as they dramatize it in the game.

Concept: Electricity Flows Along Metal Conductors and Will Not Flow Along Nonmetal Conductors as Glass or Rubber
Activity: Keep Away

If there is a large number of children, they should form a circle. For a small group the children may spread out and form a square or five-sided figure. One child is chosen to be *it,* and he stands in the center. The other children throw a ball around the circle or across the square. They try to keep the ball away from *it* while he tries to get his hands on it. If *it* catches the ball, he changes places with the last child who threw it, and the game continues. If *it* is unable to get hold of the ball in a minute's time, another *it* can be chosen.

Application:

The ball becomes the electricity, the ball throwers are the conductors, and *it* is a nonconductor who tries to interfere with the flow of electricity. Any time the nonconductor is successful in interfering, the current of electricity is interrupted. Children can be encouraged to find out the kind of materials that are non-conductors and several safety practices that have developed for those working around electricity, both in business and around the home.

Concept: A Magnet Attracts Iron and Steel
Activity: Link Tag

The children are scattered about the play area. Two children are chosen to be the Taggers. The taggers link hands and attempt to tag other children. All children tagged link hands between the first two Taggers, the chain growing longer with each addition. Only the end children, the original Taggers, may tag other children. Runners may crawl under the chain to escape being tagged, but any child who deliberately breaks the chain is automatically caught. The game continues until all the children are tagged. The last two children caught become the Taggers for the next game.

Application:

The Taggers are the magnets, and the other children represent things made of iron or steel. As the Taggers touch the other children by tagging, the children are attracted to them and become a part of the magnetic chain. It should also be pointed out that only the Taggers at the ends of the chain can tag others which demonstrates that magnets are strongest at the ends or poles.

Concept: The Force of a Magnet Will Pass Through Many
     Materials
Activity: Hook-on Tag

One child is selected as a runner or magnet. The remaining

children form groups of four. The children in each group stand one behind the other, each with arms around the waist of the child in front. The runner attempts to hook on at the end of any line where he can. The group members twist and swing about, trying to protect the end of their line from being caught. If the runner is successful, the leader of that group becomes the new runner. The group having the most of its original members in it at the end of a specified period of time is the winner.

Application:

Before starting the game, it should be pointed out that the runner in the game is the magnet. When he is successful in hooking on to the end of one of the groups, the power of the magnet travels through the group to the first person, and becomes the new magnet. This activity dramatizes that a magnet does not have to be in direct contact with another magnetic material in order to attract it. Later, children can be encouraged to experiment to determine which materials the force of a magnet will travel through.

Concept: Unlike Poles of a Magnet Attract Each Other

Activity: North And South

The class is divided into two equal groups. The two groups line up facing each other about ten feet apart midway between designated goal lines. One group is named North and the other one South. The teacher has a ten-inch square of cardboard which has *N* on one side and an *S* on the other. The teacher throws the cardboard into the air between the teams where all can see it as it lands. If the *S* side shows, the South team turns and runs to their goal line, chased by the North team. All who are tagged before reaching the line join North, and the two groups line up facing each other again. The cardboard is thrown in the air again, and the game continues in the same manner. The team which eliminates the other wins the game.

Application:

The two groups represent the opposite or unlike poles of a magnet the *N* and *S* poles. When one group turns to run to its goal line, it *attracts* the other group which pursues it.

Concept: When a Magnet Attracts an Object, That Object Becomes a Magnet

Activity: Magnet, Magnet

The children are divided into groups called Pins, Needles, Paper Clips, or anything else that can be attracted by a magnet. The groups stand behind a line at one end of the play area. One child is selected to be the Magnet and stands in the center of the play area. The Magnet calls "Magnet, Magnet. I dare Pins come over" (or any of the other groups), whereupon all the children of that group run to the opposite side of the play area. Magnet tries to catch them. Any child tagged must then help Magnet whenever he calls another group to come over. The Magnet may dare everybody over at one time or two groups at a time. The last child caught becomes the new Magnet.

Application:

The children should note that the magnet, as he tags other children, causes them to become *magnetized* and have the power to magnetize others by tagging them. The magnet *attracts* others by calling to them.

Concept: Sound Carries Through the Air

Activity: Stoop Tag

The children form a circle by joining hands. One child is *it* and stands in the center of the circle. The children walk around the circle singing:

> I am happy! I am free!
> I am down! You can't catch me!

At the word *down* the children stoop and let go of hands. Then they stand up, jump and hop about, daring the child who is *it* to tag them. They must stoop to avoid being tagged. If a child is tagged when he is not stooping, he becomes *it*.

Application:

After the children have played the game, the teacher can discuss the sounds they have heard, for example, singing, shouts, squeals. The teacher can question the children as to how these sounds got to them. It can be pointed out the sounds were sound waves traveling through the air.

Health

Concept: The Skin Is the First Line of Defense of the Body Against Infectious Agents

Activity: Body Rebels

In the center of a large play area a circle with a three-foot radius is drawn. One child is chosen to be the Body and stands in the center of the circle. Four children are selected to be the Skin and stand outside the circle. The other children are Bacteria and station themselves about the playing area nearer the boundary lines than the Skin. The Bacteria try to run past the Skin, gain entrance to the circle, and tag the Body. If the Body is tagged, the game ends, and the child who tagged the Body becomes Body for the next game. If a Skin tags a Bacterium as he tries to get into the circle to reach the Body, the Bacterium must go to a boundary line, stand still, and count to twenty before he may continue to play. The Skin try to tag the Bacteria only when they are near the circle. Once a Bacterium enters the circle, he is safe to tag the Body.

Application:

In this game the children can dramatize that the body tries to resist invasion of bacteria into the body. The skin tries to protect the body from infection. The germs are the infectious agents that sometimes get into the body, causing illness. It can also be pointed out that as long as the skin remains intact, it wards off harmful disease agents and prevents infection from entering the body. The children can be encouraged to find out how breaks in the skin are taken care of to prevent bacteria entering the body.

Concept: When One Moves or Is Exercising, the Blood Circulates More Rapidly Than When One Is at Rest

Activity: Circle Pass

The children arrange themselves in a circle. The group then counts off by two's. The number one's face inward and the number two's face outward, that is, one's and two's are facing each other. Two team captains are selected and stand opposite each other in the two circles in which the two teams are facing each other. On a signal each captain begins passing a ball around to each member of the team. The first team to get the ball around the circle back to the captain wins.

Application:

In this game the ball represents the blood, and its traveling around the circle represents the circulation of the blood through the body. The team that passes the ball around faster wins the game. Here it might be seen that the faster the physical exertion or exercise (passing the ball around), the faster the blood (the ball) circulates. The children might be considered veins, arteries, or capillaries to make the analogy more real.

Concept: Materials Are Transported Around the Body by the Circulatory System

Activity: Beanbag Pass

The children form a circle. The children take one step back so they are separated from each other by a space. Every other child should have a beanbag. On a signal each child turns toward his right-hand neighbor, tosses his bag to him, and then turns at once to receive the beanbag which is being passed to him from the left. The game should move rapidly. When the tossing has gone once or twice around the circle to the right, the direction should be changed to the left. It is good to have one of the bags a different color from the others so as to know when the circle has been completed. When the children become proficient in this form of game, more beanbags may be added until all children but one have a bag.

Application:

The beanbags represent the different materials in the body, and the circle is the circulatory system. The beanbags begin passed around the circle are materials being transported through the body by the circulatory system. Children can be encouraged to find out what kinds of materials are carried throughout the body by the circulatory system.

Concept: Organs Are Groups of Tissues Working Together To Perform Major Functions in the Body

Activity: Body Relay

Several single circles are formed. The captain of each circle holds a ball. On a signal the captain passes the ball to the right. The ball continues around the circle until it returns to the captain, who immediately raises his hand. The team finished first scores a point. Variations can be used:

Pass to the left.

Pass the ball around the circle three or four times.

Change the type of passes.

Increase the size of the circle to make passes longer.

Application:

The circles can be designated as the heart, lungs, or other organs of the body. Each child can be compared to a tissue. Just as coordination and cooperation are necessary between the children in the circles in winning the game, so these same qualities are necessary for tissues in order that the organs can perform their functions. The variations in the game may suggest that just as some of the skills are more difficult to perform than others, so are some of the functions of the organs of the body more difficult to accomplish. But with all the tissues (and team members) working together, the difficult tasks can be accomplished.

Concept: A Balanced Diet for Good Health

Activity: Change Circle Relay

The children make rows behind a starting line in teams of four each. About thirty feet in front of each team, there are two circles drawn touching each other. In one of the circles, 3 ten pins or other suitable objects are placed. On a signal the first child on each team runs up to the circles and moves the pins from the first to the second circle, and then returns to the rear of his team. The second child then runs up and puts the pins back in the first circle and returns in the same manner. The first team to finish wins.

Application:

The four members of each team represent the four food groups. It can be pointed out that a well-balanced diet needs all four food groups and that these four groups can work together to make a person healthy. The teacher can help the children to see that just as all the children on a team are needed to make it a winning team, so a balanced diet is essential for good health and that every type of food is important.

INDEX